D062293

Playing Soldier: A Diatribe

Playing
Soldier

A DIATRIBE

BY FRANK GETLEIN

Holt, Rinehart and Winston

NEW YORK   CHICAGO   SAN FRANCISCO

For Stephen, who was there

Published simultaneously in Canada by Holt, Rinehart
and Winston of Canada, Limited.

Library of Congress Catalog Number: 73-118089

FIRST EDITION

SBN: 03-085063-0

Designer: Winston Potter

Printed in the United States of America

Contents

There was something decidedly unpleasant about him, sinister, at the same time absurd, that combination of the ludicrous and alarming soon to be widely experienced by contact with those set in authority in wartime.

—ANTHONY POWELL, *The Kindly Ones*

The Game Drain

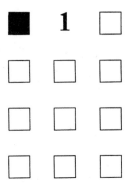

We play games, we play games, while the work of the world cries out to be done.

Homo ludens has arrived on the scene a generation early. That sporting product of affluence, freed from work, spending his days devising ways to spend his days, was billed as the man of the future. Instead, abruptly and with no one's leave, he has become the present—but the game of his choice is playing soldier.

War has always been a game to those who have played it most brilliantly, to Caesar and Napoleon, Rommel and Patton, Gustavus Adolphus and Stonewall Jackson. They have borne witness to their view and the most famous witness was borne by the man who beat Napoleon.

The battle of Waterloo, said Wellington, was won on the playing fields of Eton. In which case, a Cockney soldier might well have asked, how come the Iron Duke needed all those nonpublic school chaps to do the dying?

The battle of Waterloo was not won on the playing fields of Eton. It was won in the complex circumstances that brought about the final grand alliance against Napoleon, and it was lost in Napoleon's fatal miscalculations of his own strength. He particularly underestimated his strength relative to the enemy before the arrival of the Prussians. Had he got at the Etonians, as he should have, before the entry into battle of the soldiers who, a century later, were to be revealed as the Beasts of Berlin, Waterloo would have been quite a different thing for the Etonians. If Wellington was serious at all, Eton should have changed its games program.

Fortunately for the British Empire, Wellington wasn't all that serious. The games at Eton survived, essentially unchanged, long enough for the Etonian generals of World War I to send thousands of their countrymen to dirty death in Flanders and in France a century later.

Granted that the Great Duke was out of bounds in delivering his commercial for the Old School, granted that the principal contribution of the Etonians to the occasion was the famed Waterloo Ball, staged by Busby Berkley and starring Miriam Hopkins in a hot gavotte, still there was some small grain of truth in the Old Boy's plug for play. He just had it backwards, a common failing of military commanders of all ranks.

It wasn't that the battle was won on the playing field; it was that the battlefield, for many participants, especially those from Eton, was a marvelous extension, revival and apotheosis of the playing fields at the Old School, with the added advantage that no nurse or master's wife was ever quite in a class with Miriam Hopkins.

Waterloo was being fourteen years old again and equipped with real horses, real cannons, magnificent play clothes, toy soldiers as big as life and plenty of them, drums, banners, speed, clash, derring-do and the Waterloo Ball. Waterloo was adolescence forever, without the pimples. No wonder they loved it, those Old Etonians, looked back in sorrow for a century that it was over, and were stunned beyond recovery when the Marne and Belleau Woods turned out to be something else.

War is hell, said Sherman, who was in a good position to know, but there is a long tradition in life and letters that chooses hell over heaven because it's a livelier place. The games are better down there.

Only when we accept the game quality of war are we able to understand its universal appeal.

As a start in that direction, it is helpful to consider that war is the only presumably adult activity that has an alumni association. In fact, in the United States it has two, the American Legion and the Veterans of Foreign Wars, the latter more exclusive, the former more vociferous. There are also some splinter group alumni clubs, but they are directly or indirectly modeled on the Big Two, either adding a religious or ethnic note or attempting—futilely—to influence legislation in the opposite direction from that favored by the Big Vets.

4 □ Playing Soldier

If we really believed, as we profess to believe, that war is hell, a horrible mistake, an abomination that must not be permitted to happen again, and the rest of the standard litany, obviously there would be no powerful association dedicated to reliving the good old days of dying. The answer to this apparent paradox is games. We don't really believe all the pious antiwar litany at all. We really believe that war is a game of our youth, that it is a lot of fun, that it is to be remembered with nostalgic chuckles.

Which is pretty much the more or less official attitude of alumni associations the country over. Obeisance is occasionally made to the advancement of learning and community betterment, but in practice what an alumni association is all about is keeping up the games of yesteryear and of the new season. It is the higher learning as football. The college president, on the road for alumni contributions to the old school, is invariably accompanied by color films of last year's gridiron highlights. The big alumni events coincide with the big game and the principal service performed by the alumni association is the procurement of pairs of the coveted pasteboards, as they seem to be called, for medium to heavy alumni givers. It is an interesting and peculiarly American idea of the higher learning, and combined with the existence of war veterans' alumni associations, it is a key to the fact that war is a game and nothing else in the minds of most people involved in actually playing it—as distinguished from those who have to endure it.

The old gamesters in the veterans' organizations are

banded together for three reasons of varying shades of good or evil to themselves and their country.

The first, by far the most important and the one invariably overlooked by liberal observers who deplore vet power, is low-cost conviviality. Like most private clubs, the vet "posts" exist primarily as saloons and restaurants where the prices tend to be a little lower for members than they can get on the outside, where there are weekly specials—roast beef on Thursday, fish fry on Friday, steak on Saturday—and where local sumptuary laws can be bent a little to the extent of discreet drinking after hours and on Sundays, and, perhaps, poker tables and slot machines rigged with relative liberality.

All this, the good grub, the cheap drinks and the easy amiability of it all, is the real motivation behind the vets clubs, rather than the establishment of a Fascist dictatorship, as is often thought.

There is, to be sure, a secondary motivation operating in varying degrees of importance for various members, and this is simply to get all it is possible to get out of the federal government. In deference to this motive, the organizations operate lobbies in Washington which are, on the historical record, as effective as those of the oilmen, the doctors and the educators—that is, about as effective as lobbies get.

In times past more than at present there has been a certain amount of resentment of the veterans' raids on the treasury among citizens interested in the cause of good government. From another point of view, however, those raids, from bonuses and land grants to college educations and home loans, can be regarded as a valuable first step in the democratization of congressional largesse and in the very gradual socialization of our economic system. G.I. insurance, for example, and free medical care for veterans with service-connected disabilities are serious affronts to two of the richest and most powerful special interests in the country, the insurance industry and the medical industry, both of which tend to think of the ills of mankind as sent by God to provide a decent living for their members. Being rich, and understanding the way government works, the doctors and the insurance men have been able to hold off socialization in "their" fields for about a century longer than was possible in Europe even under such reactionary regimes as those of Bismarck and the Hapsburgs. The only substantial dent made in the wall of massive resistance to humanity in these matters was made by the veterans' organizations. If we ever do achieve anything like an adequate social welfare structure in this country, it will be in great part due to the fact that many of the specific programs needed have for years been operating on behalf of millions of veterans without the rise of an American Soviet.

So the treasury raiders aren't all bad. Surely, anyone would agree that if we are going to spend money on war rather than on more sensible things, it is better spent sending a war veteran to college or giving a pension to his widow and orphan than in buying more yachts for more board members of Lockheed and Pratt-Whitney.

Which brings up the third great area of veterans' activities, the one that gets the most notice by press and public and the least participation by actual veterans.

This is the apparent devoted effort to establish a military dictatorship in the United States by any means possible, but especially by urging Congress to give admirals and generals all they ask for in the way of money.

The phenomenon is one of the strangest in democratic life and one which can only be explained by the theory of war as games.

On the face of it, the one burning desire capable of drawing veterans together in a militant organization— roast beef and free wheel chairs aside—the one such common cause would have to be the abolition of the military establishment. It is easy for generals and admirals to buffalo Congressmen and civilian Presidents. The process is the same by which mutual fund salesmen flourish in the land. They deal in a complicated subject and the person they deal with knows little or nothing about it. Presidents particularly are pushovers for the panic approach from the Pentagon.

But veterans, as veterans, know better than that. They have seen it all from the inside. They know that the military machine is a fraud, that the military mind is deliberately self-deluded most of the time, that the military capacity for incompetence is infinite. They know all these things and they have suffered because of them. And yet, if the military tomorrow asked for funds for a system to blow up the United States to save it from the Russians, the veterans' organizations would testify to Congress the day after tomorrow that what the country needs is to be blown up and at their next conventions would pass unanimous resolutions urging that Congress stop its temporizing and get on with the dynamite.

How do you explain that?

By games and only by games. The veterans' loyalty to the Army they know all the flaws of is the alumni's loyalty to the old school. They went there and they played games. Better still, they watched games, thought about games and talked games. The games are gone, but the memory lingers on, indissolubly mixed up with the memory of their lost youth in a way that just can't be done with differential calculus or the poetry of the Augustan Age.

The alumnus responds to appeals to support the team, even when he knows that the very existence of the team casts a shadow over the presumed purpose of the school as an institution of learning. The veteran responds to the same sort of appeal even though he knows the Army is run by a crowd of megalomaniac incompetents: people incapable of ordering a nerve gas that can be handled, of running a communications system that can pass the word of a spy ship crisis, of keeping their own ships from banging into one another, or of contracting for a plane or a missile that will finally cost anywhere near the original estimates—to name at random a few of the recent achievements of Pentagon gamesmen.

If at times the veteran does indeed appear to be an "incipient Fascist," in the grand old phrase of the incipient Fascists of the lunatic left, it is really more of a vestigial desire for a return to the remembered sense of team play in the wars than any admiration for Mussolini or hope to have American trains run on time, a cause now universally recognized as lost.

The game these old soldiers remember, the game of

war, meets every definition of a game. This is not merely a matter of admirals and generals pushing counters around on maps like checkers on grids. It is very much a matter of the way everyone involved in war lives every day of his life. The game condition is at its most typical, as would be expected, among the tiny minority of men who actually fight in the wars, but it is so intense among them that its aura and atmosphere spread all the way back to mess-kit repair battalions and even to public relations regiments.

The first thing about a game is that it is an abrupt, arbitrary and deliberate removal from the ordinary work of life. It is governed by agreed-upon rules or by rules imposed whether agreed upon or not. It presents a course of action and a series of decisions. It requires the cultivation of a set of skills having very little to do with real life and often rewards sheer endurance more than any other quality of character or intellect. Perhaps the most attractive thing about a game, as compared with real life, is that it can be "won," in the sense of a successful conclusion arrived at from the point of view of one player or team which the other player or team will agree to as final, at least for that time.

By contrast, the "victories" of real life are never final and certainly never all-encompassing: there always remain other aspects of life where one's status at any moment is by no means as clear as in the one where the victory has been achieved. But the game of chess, or tennis, or golf, or gin rummy, or matching pennies, does have this gratifying element of finality. So does the game of war.

As in other games, the war player is completely insulated from reality. His artificial world is completely self-sufficient, much more so than the artificial world of golf or bridge. There is, of course, a whole scale of completeness in games, ranging from the convention of flipping coins to the more extended and elaborated conventions of golf, polo, horse and motor racing. In a few games—yacht racing, mountain climbing, big game hunting—the artificial world sustained by game conventions is actually a substantial piece of the real world, extensive enough to provide a total environment for the duration of the game. Only in war is the game total—whether the war is total or not. The game environment reaches as far as the eye can see, and goes on not merely twenty-four hours a day, as in hunting and climbing, but seven days a week, fifty-two weeks a year.

War, moreover, is extremely serious, and this is an essential attribute for any game. Like art, games begin with the willing suspension of disbelief. If you cannot contemplate the spectacle of grown men knocking little white balls about a stretch of specially prepared landscape without bursting into laughter—a common-sense reaction—you will never know the joys of golf, said to be exhilarating, exasperating and therapeutic. War, after all, is a matter of life and death. For most of us, however ridiculous a situation may be objectively, if our lives are at stake, we suspend our disbelief quite willingly, and take it quite seriously.

Taking it seriously, the combat soldier soon finds that the game depends very much on team play. It would be absurd to compare the team spirit of an infantry squad with that of a ballet company or even that of a football team as far as coordinated precision, grace and ensemble work are concerned. But on another level the same kind of cooperation keeps the group going under combat conditions and provides both the loyalty that is mistakenly thought to be generated by devotion to the free enterprise system or even to the Bill of Rights, and the morale mistakenly thought to be generated by annual visits from Bob Hope.

It is sweet and fitting to die for one's country, said the Roman poet, but he was already a propagandist for a big power. The only *patria* now in business capable of generating that authentic reaction among the people actually called upon to die is Israel. This is so because of a lot of reasons but surely one of them is size. Israel is small enough for one to be a member of, as one is a member of a family. In big power armies, the *patria* with a similar effect is the squad, possibly the platoon, if the platoon leader happens to have a rare combination of leadership talents which are mostly eliminated by the Army's system of selection and training of leaders. As a member of a small group of men, a soldier really will lay down his life for the sake of his comrades. It happens every day. So the game of war has to be serious.

But it is also nonserious. It is, for the soldier called upon to serve, an extended holiday from real life, just as a yacht race or a mountain climbing expedition is, only more dangerous and a lot more boring. This is the second essential characteristic of a game, its unreality.

In real life there are certain elemental demands that most of us have to meet every day as a matter of absolute necessity. We have to eat and drink, we have to have clothes to wear, and we have to have a place to live. In military service these are all provided, without a thought by the recipient. He does not have to worry about procuring the money to pay for these essentials, as he does in real life. He doesn't even have to concern his mind about a choice of style or menu or interior decor. These questions are all answered for him before they even arise. The deliberate removal of the player from real-life questions of decision continues through every aspect of his life in the game of war. The ideal condition, from the point of view of those who run the game, is that the individual player will make no decisions at all—unless and until something goes wrong and someone has to be presented to the public—the game audience—as responsible. At such moments, responsibility rests with the lowest possible rank, preferably a private, but a noncommissioned officer is acceptable. Barring such unavoidable accidents, however, the game is supposed to be run by its own rules and responsibility always to be bucked up the chain of command until it disappears somewhere between the communications center and the assistant secretary for press agentry.

Games, of course, have changed enormously in America in the last generation, and the game of war has changed right along with the less intensive games. Thanks to the miracle of television, it has become possible to be a totally committed gamesman without ever leaving one's comfortable armchair, except to get a cold beer or go to the bathroom during commercial announcements.

War has followed professional football and baseball onto the home screen as a spectator sport. It does not command the same amount of time in the season, but, on the other hand, it is right in there, blasting away, every night, on the news all the year round, not just weekends in the season. War even generates its television specials from time to time and, through association with leading television personalities, has taken on a little of the glamour of the tube.

From the point of view of any conscientious critic of the performing arts, it must be acknowledged that the war in Indochina has been singularly disappointing. Somehow, in the early days of World War II, before America's entry, radio broadcasts from London made that war ever so much more satisfactory as broadcast entertainment than Vietnam has ever been, except for that moment of high drama at Dien Bien Phu—again, before America's entry. Both World War II and Korea were infinitely more satisfactory in the old system of visualization, namely the drawing of colored lines upon simplified maps, than Vietnam has managed to be in the new system, television.

The reason, obviously, is that Vietnam, as our first major television war, has naturally taken on the tone and the characteristics of the dominant television manifestation, which is neither the professional game nor the comedy hour, but the soap operas which drag their repetitive, dreary way through hour after hour of every day.

Only in terms of soap opera can we understand, for instance, the regular appearance of the joint chiefs of staff—men of some intelligence, after all—assuring us once more that there is "light at the end of the tunnel," or that "the corner has been turned," or ritually repeating similar trite phrases. They are taking the place, obviously, of the famous brain surgeon or eyesight specialist who is periodically flown in from Boston—for some reason Boston has all the surgeons in televisionland—to operate on the heroine (or her husband), who has been seized by a mysterious illness. He appears outside the operating room with just the tired optimism of the joint chiefs, pats the heroine or her sister on the shoulder and says, "I think it's going to be all right now." All the joint chiefs lack in their biennial reports is a tremulo on the organ fading into the commercial spot.

Like soap opera, the Vietnam war is endless and hard to follow. You cannot come in anywhere and expect to pick it all up. Characters come and go, like joint chiefs moving in from the field and out to retirement, or like commanders in chief, for that matter, explaining that their only desire is to get our boys back but we have to keep our boys over there in order to protect our boys who are over there. It's the same language, the same incredibly circular reasoning that follows doomed heroines every day from career triumphs to mysterious ailments to adulterous temptations. There is no more reason to imagine that the war in Indochina will end than "Edge of Night" or "The Secret Storm" will end. All three have within them the seeds of immortality. Like the amoeba, they go on forever because they have no form.

Vietnam brought war as games to another sort of grand climax. We Americans have often played the diplomacy of war as if it were seven-card stud poker. We have often played war itself as if it were football or even basketball. Vietnam is the first time we—or perhaps anyone else—have played war as a game of dominoes.

The domino game in Southeast Asia has been explained to Americans by too many Presidents and their spokesmen to need repetition now. The theory is that if one domino is knocked over, it will, in falling, knock over all the others. Therefore, any sensible domino player rallies all his forces to the support of the first domino, which has been variously the regime of President Diem and Madame Nhu and that of President Thieu and Vice President Ky in South Vietnam.

There have been two basic troubles with this game of dominoes. In the first place, you don't play dominoes like that at all. Dominoes are played by matching the pips on the pieces and the object is to get rid of all your pieces, an endeavor, it must be acknowledged, in which we have received an enormous amount of help from high-ranking officials in our various domino governments.

Secondly, while we have been playing dominoes, the enemy, the North Vietnamese and their allies within the other Indochinese countries, have been playing something else. They've been playing, naturally, the ancient Asiatic game of Go, a game which consists of operating with a large number of unstructured pieces over an immense, unstructured board, the object being to surround enemy pieces anywhere and to command bits and pieces of the terrain anywhere, with no reference at all to normal lines of division between opposing forces.

That's why the war has been so strange. The opposing forces are playing entirely different games and the game they are playing is somehow much more suitable to the field than the one we are.

But we have achieved our moments of gamely importance, items for the record books to be talked about for decades by gamesters in bars. Of these, almost certainly, the highest was President Nixon's "incursion" into Cambodia in 1970, followed by an excursion of the Cambodian Communist armies all over the country and by the beginning of the systematic reduction of Cambodia to rubble by the American Air Force. It was the first time anyone ever played three-dimensional dominoes.

Name and Rank

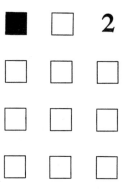

In America, to change your name is to change your luck. For many, it's part of the process of upward mobility; historically, it was part of Americanization, which for whites often seemed an almost identical process. On Ellis Island, gateway to the sweet land, the upwardly mobile from Eastern Europe or the Mediterranean were uniformly equipped with new names, thought to be Anglo-Saxon versions of their old ones, by the upwardly mobile Irish officials who had got here first.

The process was continued by the immigrants' children. It wasn't that Milton was a better name than

Moishe—Milton himself would have recoiled in horror from the comparison—but it didn't have to be explained and spelled out.

Because of this background, unique among the nations, we Americans did not react with extreme suspicion and even alarm when, in the aftermath of World War II, the War Department decided to change its name to the Department of Defense. We should have.

In addition, there is another American tradition which happened to be enjoying a revival and vogue at the time, the change of name as a means of lending a little class to a trade or occupation. Earlier in the century, undertakers had become morticians. Garbage collectors were sanitation men. Press agents became public relations consultants. Typists were converted into Girl Fridays, or Girls Friday, the plural being uncertain. Tract housing speculators, of all people, became home builders, of all things.

With garbage collectors and press agents thus classing themselves up, who could object to the poor old War Department's doing the same? After all, the military establishment had just come through the successful prosecution of World War II, not getting in the way too much of the civilians who actually fought the war in the field and won it in the factories, providing the accepted military channels and procedures which proved a stimulating challenge to all—invaluable training for outwitting the enemy. It wasn't as if the generals suddenly wanted to call themselves field marshals. That would have been militarism and America never would have stood for it. They just wanted to change the name of their game from War to Defense and why not?

Indeed, there seemed to be every reason for the change, and it had widespread civilian support and total civilian acceptance. The recently ended war had brought its own special forms of hell, not only in the evils endured by our soldiers in combat and in noncombat, but also in the evil loosed by our country in the form of the two atom bombs dropped on Japan to end the war in the Pacific. After World War I, we had all vowed never to go to war again, it was too horrible. But after World War II, there was a new and special reason for renascent pacifism. For the first time in our history a large number of Americans felt that their country had been guilty of sin in wartime. Before that, sin had been a special province of all those other people, Germans mostly, but also the Italians in Ethiopia and the Spanish insurgents in Spain. Now we ourselves were guilty and the obvious expiation was to ensure that war would never occur again.

To that end we invented the United Nations and, astonishing as it now seems, actually expected that organization to keep the peace somehow. With the same end in view, we joyfully embraced the idea of changing the name of the War Department to the Department of Defense. We believed then and, on the record, still do, that if a thing has no name it has no existence. Malinowski, no doubt, has described this or similar beliefs in the Trobriand Islands. At any rate, it has worked as well for us as it has for the Trobriand Islanders. No longer having the name War as part of the government, we no longer have wars. Instead we have police actions, as in Korea, advisory services, as in Vietnam, where we also have Vietnamization, and incursions, as in Cambodia. We have thus eliminated wars completely except for the people who have to fight them and the people who have to suffer them being fought across their fields, through their villages, and over their dead bodies.

Their turn will be next. You have to begin somewhere, and we began with the name.

The trouble with this approach is not so much that it conceals the truth. Hiding the truth is frequently, perhaps usually, the only way to live with it. We all do it all the time. But it is essential, when you hide the truth, to know that you have hidden it, to know where you have hidden it, and to remember what it is. This is not really difficult. It is done every day of their lives by governors of the Federal Reserve, television executives, ordinary philanderers, theologians and the better Pop singers, to name a few. You only get into trouble when you hide the truth and forget where you've put it and what it is. That's what we did with our all-new Department of Defense.

The error was fairly gross. You don't really have to change the name of War Department to Defense Department in order to have all your wars be wars of defense. Has anyone ever fought any other kind?

Well, yes, a few peoples have at one time or another. The Vandals, the Lombards, the Visigoths and the Ostrogoths, the Teutons and the Huns, all fought widespread and disastrous wars just for the hell of it—the principal secret reason for wars—and in order to grab the lands and treasure of other people, the leading secondary reason. But about everyone else has fought strictly for defense.

The Romans defended themselves so well they established defense points and walls all over Europe, the Middle East and North Africa. Hitler defended the Germans from Stalingrad to the Atlantic, from the North Pole to the Sahara. He also defended his people from the Jewish threat by killing six million Jews. In the same war, the Soviets defended the Russian people from the aggressive designs of the Finns, and have since defended them from the Czechs, the Hungarians, the Poles and the East Germans, not to mention the Latvians, Estonians and Lithuanians, all of whom, apparently, have posed grave threats to the continued existence of the Soviet motherland, a more delicate organism than it looks.

We ourselves, if it comes to that, got into the big-time self-defense business in similar ways. We took Cuba to defend the Panama Canal and we took Panama to defend California, which is fundamentally indefensible. Inexplicably, we turned Cuba loose and hung onto the Philippines for decades despite the proximity of Cuba to the Canal and the demonstrable distance between Manila and Malibu, to say nothing of the infinitely better record at self-government of Asiatics over Spanish Americans. We did these things through a War Department and a Navy Department and we did them strictly for self-defense. We wouldn't have dreamed of doing them for aggrandizement. Any aggrandizing that happened was just one of those crazy things.

In other words, you don't really have to change the name of the government department in order to fight wars solely for defensive purposes. Those are the only purposes civilized countries ever do fight wars for, the capacity for such self-deception being one of the most basic characteristics of civilization.

But there are older traditions of name-changing than those of turning in Wishniewski for a new-model Wisher and upgrading the town by calling the swimming pool the natatorium. It is on those older traditions that we ran aground in the grand switch from the aggressive old War Department to the pleasant, amiable, thoroughly commendable Defense Department.

In the older tradition there are two kinds of people who go around changing their names, the holy and the crooked. The Defense Department has turned out to be both, and it is isn't surprising to anyone familiar with either the Bible or the Annals of Crime and Rascality.

Judaism begins with Abram, citizen of Ur, changing his name to Abraham, as a sign of his personal convenant with God. Since the Old Testament never does anything once if it can do it twice, Abraham's grandson Jacob had his name divinely changed to Israel. The beginning of Christianity is also highlighted by a change of name, Simon into Peter, and since then, monks, nuns and popes all change their names as a sign of their union with God.

On the other hand, Giuseppe Balsamo changed his name to Count Cagliostro and became probably the greatest swindler in the eighteenth century—against a lot of first-class competition. An Irish army brat a century later changed her name to Lola Montez and became not only a famed Spanish dancer but for a time the effective ruler of Bavaria.

The newly named Defense Department can only be

understood in that older tradition. It became at once Cagliostro, Lola Montez, and the strong right arm of God. Like Cagliostro, it dabbled deeply in alchemy and persuaded all sorts of innocents that it had plumbed the secrets of the universe. Like Lola, it became a professional seducer of monarchs. Like Abraham, Israel and most popes, it came on like the voice of God explaining his business in the world. Like most of those who do God's business for him, the Defense Department has never had any great problem sorting out its own concerns from those of the divinity: it is easier to assume they are identical.

The difference between War Department and Defense Department is one of scope. Everyone knows what a War Department is supposed to do. It is supposed to make war when that is called for by the people to whom the War Department reports; when it is not making war it is supposed to be getting ready to make war by such accepted measures as close order drill and gunnery practice.

A Department of Defense is something else again. It is charged, by title, with a mission of defending the country, a mission which is not particularly well defined, against all enemies, a term even less sharply defined. Making war, if not easy, at least allows everyone involved to know what it is. To defend the country is larger, vaguer, more comprehensive and at the same time less susceptible of limitation of any kind. It is exactly the sort of mission sought by people like Cagliostro and arrogated by people like popes. It's a permanent, all-season hunting license with no place out of bounds.

If the military mission is to make war, the military

establishment, somewhat like the Vice President, stands and waits until circumstances and the proper, elected authorities tell it that the moment has come to make the war. Result: happiness.

If, on the other hand, the military mission is to defend the country, then the military establishment is derelict in duty if it merely waits for the word; on the contrary, it must go out and meet threats in their infancy, long before they become full-blown, and without too much worry about whether they will become full-blown if left alone; without, for that matter, a great deal of concern as to whether the threats really exist at all. Result: misery.

Under the second, and existing, arrangement, the military may fairly engage in all sorts of intelligence operations in friendly and unfriendly nations. If these operations detect the possibility of a threat to American defense, the military may and should create, and or encourage, clandestine resistance movements against governments thought to be potentially unfriendly. To such movements the military may sell or give arms, ammunition and actual troops in various disguises or, eventually, in none at all. In such ways can wars begin without anyone having to trouble Congress to declare them.

It should surprise no one that if wars can begin in that way, they have begun in that way. For the people responsible for beginning them, the military, are also the people who stand to gain most from this country's being at war. It is probably true that no one in charge of the military consciously desires war for the sake of war. There are too many other good reasons, most of them variations on the defense of America. But still, when war comes and the rest of us are inconvenienced, dislocated and distressed by its events, the military are rewarded.

Such have been the fruits of the change of name. But the change was accompanied by two other changes which have made the results even worse than the deceptive switch from War to Defense would have by itself. The first was unification of the armed services. The second was the introduction of a broad band of civilian administrative talent at the top of the newly unified military establishment.

Both changes enjoyed widespread support throughout the country. Unification, for critics of the old Army and Navy games, was a simple matter of efficiency. Soldiers and sailors alike went through a predictable number of shoelaces in the course of a year. Didn't it make sense to have them be interchangeable? If the corner supermarket offers a discount on quantity buying, doesn't the same principle apply, even more so, to the huge amounts of material needed to run armies, navies and air forces? Isn't it just more efficient to make the parts one as far as possible?

In view of the respected status of the efficiency expert in American society, the questions would seem to be purely rhetorical. They were certainly accepted as rhetorical, their answers implied in the form of the questions, and unification soon followed. But there is a reasonable answer to all such questions about efficiency in the separate and the unified armed services: it all depends on what you want to be efficient about. It is not at all crystal clear that the American tradition demands total military efficiency. There is a case to be made that military inefficiency and the divided services are just what are called for if we are to retain the American way.

Most of us are too polite today to recall it, but there is a strong element of antimilitarism throughout American history. One of George III's monstrous crimes, to begin with, was sending his troops over here and quartering them upon us. We resented them then and not enough has changed in the military-civilian relationship since that time to soften our resentment. The great flow of middle European immigrants in the middle of the nineteenth century was occasioned largely by a desire to avoid conscription. The even greater wave of ingathering from Eastern Europe at the end of that century and the beginning of this one came here in great part to get away from Czarist soldiers and their free and easy attacks on civilians. We all have our ancestral reasons for being distrustful of armies. It is not too much to believe that such ancestral mistrust was behind the old-style, nonunified separate services.

What is odd about the transition is that the people who had most to gain were the ones who were loudest in their condemnation of the change, namely the generals and admirals. They were sure it couldn't work and were always equipped with reasons why. As things have turned out, they may have been right, but from the point of view of saving the country from its military establishment, which ought to be a permanent concern of any representative government, it was the civilians who had a vested interest in military separatism. The generals had theirs in unification. Both sides, however, behaved exactly contrary to their true interests.

That situation is hardly without parallel, of course. Doctors, or at least their official spokesmen in public statements and private communications to members of Congress, have always been monumentally opposed to what they have called "socialized medicine," by which, usually, has been meant any scheme aimed at guaranteeing that people would be able to afford medical care. Yet the assorted tentative, scattered and uncertain steps toward "socialized medicine" that have been taken— Blue Cross, Blue Shield, Medicare—have had as their first, most visible effect not the raising of health conditions for Americans but the making of rich men out of American doctors. How could they have been so dense as to oppose their good fortune?

If we grant that, taken all in all, doctors tend to be better educated and more intelligent to start with than generals, it is not hard to accept the fact that generals, too, fought vigorously against the greatest aggrandizement the profession of arms has ever had in this country, the unification of the services.

It is almost enough to shake one's belief in the existence of the military-industrial complex until we remember that conspirators don't have to be smart to be conspirators. They just have to conspire.

Against their wills, kicking and screaming all the way, the generals and admirals were forced into the promised land of American arms, a state in which they speedily found themselves a separate and equal branch of the government, just like the President, the Congress and the Supreme Court.

"Divide and conquer," Julius Caesar used to say,

shortly before beginning the most critical military take-over of the ancient world. Indeed, this has always been an operating principle of tyrants seeking control of governments in other hands. The genius of the American Constitution is that, for the first time in history, the founders applied that principle, in advance, against ty-rants, against the rule of the single strong man or deter-mined group. The principle is best known in the separa-tion of powers among the three constituted branches—the Pentagon being, as yet, an unconstituted fourth. But the principle is also behind the doctrine of the separation of Church and State, which gives every man's conscience refuge from the State and every man's taste refuge from the Church. The principle was obviously embodied also in the separation of military powers, a separation so deep as to constitute competition, even hostility. There was a lot more to the Army-Navy game in the old days than a football contest. No matter which side lost, the rest of us won through the perpetuation of interservice rivalry, as it used to be called when it was thought to be bad.

In one of those footnotes to history that keep the A.P. and U.P.I. night wires going in the dead hours, it is particularly ironic that the really effective imposition of unification should have been presided over by Robert McNamara, Secretary of Defense recruited from the Ford Motor Company by John F. Kennedy, and retained by Lyndon B. Johnson until it all got too much for both of them. Ford had been brutally shoved into permanent second place in the industry by the aggressive style of General Motors not only in competition with other car companies but most especially in a deliberately fostered internal competition among the branches of the overall corporation. Chevrolet regularly attacks the Pontiac market. Oldsmobile's constant message is that it can compete on price with Pontiac and even Chevrolet. Buick goes for the Cadillac market while Cadillac is engaged in a steady effort to "upgrade" Buick buyers. However opposed to competition from without General Motors may be, the corporation is keenly aware of its value. The same kind of competition acted as a fundamental safeguard for Americans against their military establishment before unification. Now it is gone.

McNamara also introduced civilians on the grand scale. Again, in theory this ought to have been further protection of the citizens against the military. In practice it worked exactly the other way around because the civilians took the whole thing seriously in a way the old soldiers never did, whatever their rank. Oh, an occasional MacArthur would think himself God or an occasional Patton would think himself John Wayne, but by and large our ancient professional army, top to bottom, had few delusions of grandeur in the great world. Officers and enlisted men alike had, in that comforting phrase, found a home in the Army—or a snug harbor in the Navy. Getting accepted as a recruit, or getting, by one means or another, a commission, was rather like getting elected President if you were Richard Nixon. There was nothing in particular you wanted to do with the squad, the platoon, the division, the brigade or the Army Group that you commanded. Command was an end in itself and a boat not to be rocked. It was poetry, really, in the modern formulation of a very old thought about poetry: "A poem should not mean, but be." That bit of aesthetic insight explains everything you don't understand about the Nixon Administration and it also sums up the supreme virtue of the old Army and Navy. Just being there was all there was.

We have changed that and we have done so at our peril. The effect on learning alone is a fair enough measure of the cost to society of the new military efficiency. In the olden times—1942, to be specific—the scientists of America humbly petitioned the Commander in Chief to put up a little dough to see if they couldn't split the atom and make some new kind of bomb. How incredible this now seems! Nowadays the Department of Defense, in the routine pursuits of its mission, thinks up possible threats to the country and farms out the problems to selected universities, charging them to find the costly answers if they love their country and their grants. As any wild-eyed Weatherman, bomb in hand, will be glad to tell you, the change has profoundly changed the university itself.

In foreign affairs, time was (and not so long ago) when the main contribution of the old War Department to this interesting field of human endeavor was to furnish, to our major embassies, presentable field grade officers known as military attachés, whose function was to make decorative appearances at dinners and dances in foreign climes. The actual conduct of foreign affairs, it went without saying, was in the hands of professional diplomats reporting to politically appointed ambassadors. No more. The military abroad are now charged with defense, not dancing, and the results have been disaster in South

America and Asia, which may yet prove to have been the out-of-town tryouts.

All of this is monstrous and not to be borne. We are bearing it.

If ever the military-industrial-academic-congressional-labor union complex is brought under control by the people who now, willy-nilly, support it in its megalo-maniacal style, it will be first of all by changing its name back to the cheery and modest, honest and limited title, War Department.

We shall have to admit to ourselves that the reason we have the Department is to wage war, but the last quarter century's experience with the classier cognomen should have prepared us to face that depressing truth.

The newly reconstituted War Department, for its part, will understand that its mission is solely to wage war when we tell it to do so and not to find itself occasions for doing so. When we do not tell it to wage war, its mission is to stand by, to move regularly about from post to post and, rather more slowly, up the ladder from grade to grade, visiting the homes of superiors and leaving behind their cards with the proper corners turned down, dancing till dawn on command, engaging in that modicum of discreet adultery inevitable in any closed society and, in general, lending a bit of color and dash to a nation which is quite bureaucratically dull enough without making a dull bureaucracy of the profession of Cyrano, D'Artagnan, George Custer and Sergeant Flagg.

War Versus Army

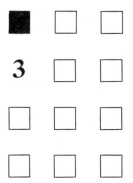

Any red-blooded American boy over the age of thirty was taught in his childhood that the United States has never lost a war. The doctrine presents one historical difficulty and one present-policy difficulty, but its adherents have managed to surmount both.

The historical difficulty is the War of 1812, a delayed replay of the Revolution fought by the British to regain their military honor and by ourselves to make the Revolution stick. Both sides won, oddly enough, which may suggest a pattern for the happy ending of future wars that refuse to halt in the traditional way.

The British won in the conventional way by piling up an almost unbroken string of military victories. Our own winning of the war took place more in the history books than on the field, through the transformation of disaster into heroic events, a process the American South was to follow to immense advantage later in the century. The rewritten scorecard reads like this: We did, after all, emerge from 1812 with New England intact and part of the Union, which hardly seemed likely when we went in; Old Hickory scored a smashing amphibious victory at New Orleans, and the fact that the victory occurred some time after the war was officially over was easily subsumed into Jackson's later triumphs over the Supreme Court and the Biddle bank; even the British burning of the new capital at Washington, the sort of event usually considered undeniable evidence of defeat, has been transformed into the attractive pastoral-epic of Dolley Madison's flight into the Virginia countryside with the White House silver and Gilbert Stuart's picture of Washington; on top of all that, while the British were beating the daylights out of Baltimore, the *Star Spangled Banner* got composed by an eyewitness to the catastrophe. How could a war with all those good things in it be called a defeat?

The rest of the martial tale has been victory pure and unalloyed. The reason the Civil War took so long and was so bloody was that it engaged Americans against Americans. With foreign foes, we have been more expeditious. We courageously routed the Indians, the Mexicans, and the Indians again. We defeated Spain in combined naval-land engagements halfway round the world from each other, thus ending forever the presumptuous claims of the discoverers on the hemisphere we had made our own. Within that hemisphere, from Santiago Harbor on, we regularly landed and got the situation back in hand, usually under the friendly rivalry of Pat O'Brien and Jimmy Cagney, who might also have been noticed, in those years, maintaining order in the bars of Shanghai and along the Yellow River, as part of our hemispheric defense plan.

But the great victories were the great wars, the two in this century designated "world." In both, the European powers got themselves fearfully balled up and in serious danger of losing to the Germans, a fate twice averted by the entry of the forces of the New World. Twice in a row the Boches, or Krauts, demonstrated they could best the best of the rest of the world, while the Americans demonstrated they could take the Germans. That left us as all-time champs; one more war and we keep the cup.

Not only that, but in the last engagement we moved on from the industrial production that had given us the title into the new world of techno-science and produced a bomb capable of destroying Japanese cities at the rate of one bomb, one city. The natural postwar development of that fearsome weapon has increased its power many times over, its destructive capability easily keeping up with the urban sprawl of the same period. By the mid-fifties, a single bomb could ruin not only a city, but its suburbs as well. By the middle of the Nixon Administration, as the urban sprawl was merging into megalopolis, a single shot, MIRV-ed up as required, could knock out that new complex as well. Even without abortion-on-demand and The Pill universally available, research-and-development in death-and-destruction seems easily able to pace the population explosion.

So confident, indeed, are the researchers and developers of being able to kill off all the people the earth is able to produce and then some, that they have for some time now been concentrating their efforts, instead, on machines aimed at destroying the enemy's machines rather than merely his men. The nuclear-tipped missiles are deployed all over the world, in submarines beneath the murky seas, in hardened siloes in the ground, and in aircraft ready to leap aloft at a moment's notice. The Russians, it is true, have done many of these things themselves, but, taken all in all, we do have a legitimate claim to being the greatest military power history has ever known, an odd distinction for a people who have never thought of themselves as particularly bellicose.

All this being so—the unbroken string of victories from Bunker Hill to Korea, the unmatched panoply of power from Antolia to Taiwan and back again—something very strange has been happening in Southeast Asia, and has been going on now for quite a few years. We are being fought to a standstill by a guerrilla army in sneakers with no offensive air force and very rare tanks and artillery. We have bombed them and bombed them and bombed them, but they have kept turning up to harrass our allies and ourselves as if no bomb had fallen. Evidently they have never grasped the doctrine of victory through air power.

Military apologists in the press and the Pentagon have let our leaders off the hook by explaining, first, that the enemy, the Viet Cong, was cheating by getting direct military assistance from North Vietnam. But when did North Vietnam become all that much of a military power? No one seriously pretends it is in a class with the Germanies of the Kaiser and the Führer, yet it is clobbering us as those imperial armies never did. For all-around command of the art of battle, no one on the North Vietnam general staff seems to have anything like the genius of, say, Sitting Bull, but whoever is in charge over there is running rings around us exactly as he did, although we have expended more power there than Custer and his contemporaries ever dreamed could exist.

What has happened to us?

There are two basic theories about that, both of them wrong.

Dove-ish moralists see the situation as a parable of power, citing St. Paul on the vanity of gaining the whole world and suffering the loss of one's own soul. In this view Vietnam is a detour in our national Pilgrim's Progress, not as attractive as Vanity Fair, but just as diverting from the Pilgrim's true goal, which, in these latter-day moralities, is thought to be rebuilding the slums as garden apartments, educating and compensating the American Negro for the troubles he's seen, cleaning up the water and air, and somehow reconstituting the government as a participatory democracy, whatever that may mean. Because we have blundered off the path to righteousness, we are bogged down in the slough of Vietnam. We must get out, reject all thought of victory, make amends to the memory of Ho Chi Minh, bring back the draft dodgers from Canada and Sweden, and admit them to the G.I. Bill of Rights. When we have thus expiated our military sins,

we shall be once more on the clear road to a truly liberal
government with no more police and the universities run
by the Students for a Democratic Society.

Thus is the voice of the turtle dove heard in the land.
The hawk sings a different tune.

According to the soaring inhabitants of this other
aviary, we are bogged down in Vietnam because of political interference with the military command, which is
ready, as it has always been, to win the war in about two
weeks anytime it is allowed to. The formula is simple:
saturation bombing of North Vietnam and anywhere else
the North Vietnamese and their various allies or puppets
may be lurking, including, as a minimum, the rest of
former French Indochina, and accepting, as the maximum, the possibility of blowing up China on the principle of better now than later.

What the hawks are talking about, although they
mention it only discreetly, is nuclear bombing. The problem is that, from the point of view of air war strategy,
nuclear bombs are still only a difference in degree from
conventional bombs. The air fleets that have for so long
visited ruin upon the rice fields and forests of Vietnam
north and south could have produced Hiroshima and
Nagasaki readily enough. The atom made it easier, but
it didn't make it different, as people in Dresden and Rot-
terdam will testify.

The real reason for keeping out of nukemanship in
Vietnam, as it was in Korea, is not a decent respect for
the opinion of mankind, still less pure humanitarianism,
as the hawks darkly suspect, but simply because the damn
bombs don't work. The conventional ones, in mass un-

paralleled, don't work, and the nukes wouldn't work either. You can bomb cities into total submission or total obliteration, but you cannot do the same thing to peoples of farm and forest. We ought to know because we have been trying it since 1964 in vain. You can nuke the Gooks till the water buffalo come home and it will profit you nothing if the Gooks have been so graceless as to have a society essentially pre-urban in its structure.

As for the morality play of the doves, it is an affecting little drama and right enough in its assessment of the things we lose for the sake of the war. But it has little relation to military reality. If wars were won by the righteous, none of the world's great empires would have existed and Eastern Europe would be a collection of independent countries. Our unrighteousness is no more the answer to why we are so hopeless in Vietnam than is our half-heartedness, in the military view.

The answer to the problem of the Vietnamese stalemate in the face of all our power is very simple. This is the first time the Army—any Army—has been able to keep total tabs on the War—any War. The high command can stay right in there with the low command every hour of every day, if it wants to. This is the worst possible way to fight a war. No wonder we cannot win it.

It all goes back to Bridgeport, Connecticut, more than thirty years ago. On the outskirts of that city, several times a week, the employees of the Sikorsky airframe works would crowd to the windows to chant, "Igor! Up he goes! Down he comes! Igor and his helicopter! Igor!" as their employer maneuvered his curious machine above the company parking lot for the amusement of visiting

military men. At the time the helicopter merely seemed
one of the deadends in aerial evolution—much as the
dirigible still does—but Igor has come into his kingdom
in Vietnam.

The helicopter, of course, has done inestimable good
for the soldiers. Among other things, it has reduced the
death level among battlefield casualties to an incredibly
low percentage. It has permitted a kind of commuter's
war, in which combat units fly in, fight, and fly out in
time for a favorite television program or a weekend on
the beach. It has even, in the form of the gunship, produced the kind of superartillery support that ground
soldiers always hoped for and never reliably received
from conventional aircraft.

But as Igor Sikorsky was demonstrating on that parking lot, whatever goes up has to come down. The helicopter that has eased the life of the combat soldier by keeping
him in touch with the amenities of life in the rear echelons
has also made combat success just about impossible by
allowing the Army to get right down into the War and
muck about in it in a way that no command body has ever
been able to do in the entire history of warfare. Throughout that history, a decent and necessary distance has been
maintained between the War and the Army. In Vietnam,
the helicopter has eliminated that distance and we have
seen the results on the front pages of each day's news
since the Kennedy Administration: disaster.

The common-sense school of military history has long
agreed that the principle condition that allowed for the
vast spread of the Roman Empire and its centuries of
endurance was simply the wretched state of communica-

tions in those days. A runner took weeks to get from Rome to the Rhine, longer to London. By what were rowboats, with primitive if any auxiliary sails, a message took just as long to get by water to Spain or Sparta. The fighting men could make their decisions and carry them out before headquarters at Rome could hope to get a representative on the spot.

How different today. The joint chiefs themselves and all their thrones, dominions and powers move easily by jet from Washington to Saigon, and by helicopter to anywhere in the entire field of fighting.

From time to time observers have wondered at the possible ill effects this easy dislocation in time and space may have upon the quality of command decisions. But the worst cost of the new convenience is not in finding dinner served when the body and mind cry out to sleep, nor even in getting Monday and Tuesday hopelessly entangled with each other. The worst cost is the destruction of the historical and necessary distance between the Army and the war.

The Army and the war represent two wildly different kinds of activity. Until our own time the difference was implicitly or explicitly recognized by everyone having to do with either one of them. The Army went its way, producing many groups of soldiers admirably trained to march up and down in unison and to create the illusion of psychotic neatness and cleanliness. Quite apart from all that, the War went its way, sloppy and disorganized, not really subject to the sort of regularized existence that the Army just doesn't feel comfortable without.

The Army is bureaucratic and hierarchical in its inmost soul. Neither of these characteristics is at all adaptable to combat conditions. In combat, things change from day to day, even from hour to hour, whereas both bureaucracy and hierarchy are designed to deal with unchanging, eternal verities.

There is nothing particularly wrong with the bureaucratic and hierarchical. The qualities characterize some of our great human institutions, from the Roman Catholic Church and the Supreme Soviet to the Department of Agriculture, the television networks and the AFL-CIO. But bureaucracy assumes that there is a set and prescribed way to do anything, and that this is the right and only way to do it. Hierarchy assumes that the next man up the ladder always and infallibly knows the answers to all the questions troubling those a rung or two down. These assumptions are excellent ones for finding out what Lenin would have thought about freedom of the press in Prague or what St. Peter would have thought about a married clergy, had either prophet been confronted with those threats to law and order. They are superb when it comes to making rich farmers richer still or to selecting next season's smash hit shoot-'em-up on the tube. The assumptions of bureaucracy and hierarchy are also useful enough in designing science fiction weapons for science fiction wars which, as they say, will never be fought, but which can cost so much without being fought that the fighting is superfluous. But one thing that bureaucracy and hierarchy cannot do is to fight an actual, bloody, shooting, on-the-ground war.

If there is only one right way to do something and if the hierarchical superior, by virtue of his office, is the one who knows the right way, then any suggestion from below that there is another way is not only wrongheaded, it is against the natural order of things and is, in a word, treason. This hierarchical principle was behind the celebrated court-martial of Billy Mitchell, the premature aviation nut. Mitchell was so early that he came into existence as an aerial soldier before there was a corresponding bureaucracy and hierarchy of air warfare, with the result that the poor man not only had to work it all out himself but also automatically be in disgrace with generals higher in the Army hierarchy who had not thought these things up for themselves. A capital crime. An infantryman, whose trade is as old as warfare, would have known better. He would have done what had to be done and lied to his superiors, explaining that what had been done to achieve victory was exactly what was prescribed in the manuals so helpfully published by the military hierarchy and bureaucracy. That kind of mutual understanding between War and Army over the centuries is what kept both in business. The Vietnam debacle, caused by the Army's insistent abrogation of the ancient, if unwritten, treaty, is more serious than the Vietnam war, distressing as that is. The pattern established may mean the end of War itself, with military exercises hereafter inevitably bogged down in the mess that naturally results when Wars are allowed to be managed by Armies.

George Bernard Shaw summed up a lot about the whole question of War and the Army when he observed that war was much too important a matter to be left in the hands of generals. In fact, of course, war never was left in the hands of generals. It was carried on instead by captains, lieutenants and, especially, sergeants and private soldiers. In Vietnam, almost for the first time, generals are able to get involved in combat affairs and they are giving war a bad name.

Consider the matter of the Body Count, which is what our generals have given us in Vietnam instead of the old-time battle maps with their red and blue underlines and curving arrows. The Body Count is a natural Army idea. It fits into the already-existing bureaucratic mechanism of the Morning Report, and more than any element in the traditional Morning Report is subject to the most blatant lying to make the reality of War seem to accord with what the Army obviously wishes were true. At the published rates of the Body Count, surely we have, on paper, killed all the available able-bodied men of military age in North Vietnam long ago and are now working our way through the second muster of the entire military population. The predictable problem is: How many times will our generals be content with killing each and every enemy?

In addition to inventing the Body Count in Vietnam as a measure of progress and a new version of the old-time annual Tall Story Contest of the American West, the Army, unleashed in Vietnam as it had never been in previous wars, has come up with two special devices almost guaranteed to lose wars.

The Army has grumbled from time to time that the draft for Vietnam has severely limited the freedom of action of the military command and thus—along with so many other impediments from the frightful "politicians" and civilians generally—not allowed the Army to

win the war as it could so easily if not crippled by the
humanitarians. The theory is clear enough. In contrast
to the olden times, when young men were drafted for the
duration, candidates for Vietnam have been drafted for
two years. The Pentagon complains—not in its own person, but through its assorted voices in the press and in—
perish forbid—politics, that in two years a soldier just
about has the hang of things and there he goes back to
civilian life, leaving the poor old Army with new drafted
men to train all over, shove into the line, and hope for the
best.

The argument made a certain amount of superficial
sense to anyone who failed to understand what the Army
was really doing in Vietnam, namely, aggrandizing itself
and its hard-core members at the considerable expense of
the nation. After all, experience in any line of work is the
golden qualification for which there is no substitute, and
so on in that line for several paragraphs.

Then, in the summer of 1970, the Army announced,
with no special fanfare, that it was discontinuing an
established policy whereby combat soldiers could get out
of combat by signing up for a three-year hitch in the
Army. The pattern, questioning revealed, was that after
drafted citizens had been through their basic training in
the States and were about three months into their agreed-
upon one year in 'Nam, they were offered the chance to
get out of combat permanently in return for signing on
for another three years in the Army. Those who valued
their lives more than their liberty did indeed sign on and
moved back to the rear. Their places were taken by replacements from the States and the war went on, as it

had, in an amateurish, catch-as-catch-can way while the new people learned the ropes. As soon as they had learned the ropes, they, too, were offered the chance to split out of combat to the rear echelons or even back to "the world" of the States in return for an extra three years.

It is difficult to take the situation seriously without proposing that anyone remotely responsible for the procedure be shot out of hand.

Yet the Army, in announcing the end of the program, did not apologize. Quite the contrary, the tone of the announcement was basic general-officer sullenness: The reason for dropping the program was that the withdrawal of a miniscule number of troops in Vietnam plus the announced decrease of drafted soldiers had made it impossible for the Army to go on giving its hostage citizens a chance to save their lives. Tough on them, the Army said, but don't blame us. It added: Well, no more Mr. Nice Guy.

At a minimum, the discarded procedure of remitting a man's statutory combat service was extortion, blackmail and kidnap ransom. But from the forgotten viewpoint of how to win a war, it was the much more serious crime of sacrificing combat efficiency for the sake of building up the numbers of regular army volunteers, three-year men, some of whom could be counted on, after the three, to stick around on the ground that so much of one's life had been shot that another fifteen years to retirement might as well follow. While it was following, however, meanwhile back at the front, the war was tossed into the hands of the new recruits and good luck to them.

It is hard to imagine a more deliberate way for an army to cripple itself.

Yet, hard as it is to imagine, the Army tried. At the same time that the Army in Vietnam was crippling itself by deliberately offering experienced combat veterans a chance to reduce their accepted combat service by seventy-five percent, the Army was also crippling itself in the officer class. The motivation here was the other way around but the effect was exactly the same, to guarantee that the combat units were always inexperienced and hence ineffective. Again, it almost surpasses belief.

The officer ploy was promotion. The experience of combat, in the Army, is mystical rather than practical. For a career officer, at a certain age and rank during the 1960s and 1970s, it is essential to his future progress that he have on his record a tour of duty in Vietnam, the big combat jamboree of the day. It is further essential, if he hopes to break through field grade into general officership, that he command a combat unit. For this reason and for this reason alone, combat command in Vietnam has been operated as a revolving door or a fraternity initiation. To make room for the next bunch of career-happy "pledges," command has been pretty generally limited to six months' time. Like Igor in his flying machine, in they come, out they go, and nobody is ever really on top of his job. By the time he is, he has to move on to make room for the next joint chief of the future.

Both these systems comprise, apparently, an excellent way to run the Army, but they are no way at all to run a war.

The Italian front, in the second of the world wars of

the first half of our century, was an ideal place to study the differences between the War and the Army. Between brief, rather frantic periods of advance, the fighting line tended to be stabilized for considerable periods. Each time it was newly stabilized, by amazing coincidence, the logical emplacement and bivouac positions for the Americans turned out to be right on the receiving end of pre-zeroed-in German artillery, a condition not without its hardships but one which, in compensation, did cut front-line visits from rear-echelon brass to an absolute minimum. The War was thus enabled to continue in its own sloppy, unmilitary way, while, back in North Africa, back in Caserta, back in Rome, back, back, back, the Army was free to work its will on its subjects, keeping them clean-shaved, sharply-pressed, properly deferential to their betters, and immaculately safe from the dirt and disorder of combat.

This natural division of spheres of activity was generally satisfactory to both sides. The Army complained about the bad example set by combat soldiers allowed back into Armyland for little holidays or "schools," another device used to maintain the compromise between War and Army. The War people, for their part, complained of the difficulty in getting the equipment and supplies needed to carry on the war.

The Army solved its psychological problem by the occasional arrest of a combat soldier in town who looked particularly unkempt or insubordinate. The charges were invariably quashed, since the combat man was quite willing to accept the safety of a rear-echelon jail in exchange for the daily danger of death up front and everyone knew it, but the motions of arrest and the sending of papers back and forth made the Army feel it was doing its part in not letting the War interfere with its ritual observances of military discipline.

On the other side, the War folk solved their problem by theft. The favored technique was to drive to a supply dump in the middle of the night in a party of at least three and preferably four men in a jeep with trailer, flim-flam the officer in charge, avoid the more knowledgeable sergeant and make off with what was needed. In this way the War got fought in spite of Army Tables of Organization designed to fight some other war, especially one on the blackboards of the Command and General Staff School.

The Army, however, struck back regularly in the form of visits from the Inspector-General, a function precisely captured by Gogol in his comedy of that name. On these occasions, in honor of which combat units were pulled back to rear areas more in keeping with the lifestyle of general officers, all equipment and material was counted and the unit was expected to have no more and no less than was clearly printed in the Tables of the Law.

Authorized equipment, received and thrown away because useless, was immediately stolen from the nearest supply dump, by means of the usual flim-flammery against innocent young lieutenants of the rear echelon. Unauthorized but acquired equipment was buried in a large pit dug for the purpose, over which a heavy truck was parked during the official Visitation. The ceremonial inspection accomplished, the stolen equipment was thrown away and the buried equipment replaced by new thievery. It was a great deal of unnecessary work for all, but it allowed, on the one hand, the Army to imagine it was prosecuting the war according to the command- ments and, on the other, it allowed the war to be fought. These are the compromises men live by.

One more instance from that laboratory situation of War and Army side by side. The Italian war ended, as all things must. The Allied troops swept down out of the Apennines for the last time, into the Emilian plain. There was fighting along the Po and some more in Verona, mostly due to German units not having received the word from their own rear echelons, but except for such familiar incidents, the last campaign was a romp, a walk to the river and then to the mountains and the war's end in the lush Italian springtime.

Abruptly, in the midst of this pastoral idyl, something foreign intruded. It was the rear echelon. It was the Army. With the sound of horns and motors, colonels of triplicate typing and brigadiers of filing cabinets ap- peared upon the scene, having heard of the easy cam- paign and seizing the chance to pick up a few authentic battlefield souvenirs for free instead of at the mark-up they usually had to pay the combat men. Up the dusty roads they came churning in their staff cars and suntan uniforms, forcing the walking soldiers off to the side and covering them with new layers of dust.

The dust, however, also caught the distant attention of a vagrant battery or two of the German artillery and they began lobbing a few in. The walking soldiers, in auto- matic reaction, threw themselves into the roadside ditches and lay there. The Army people, in reaction no less automatic, refused to soil their pretty clothes and stayed in the road, turning their staff cars about for a grand retreat and, in the process, getting quite a few of themselves and their vehicles banged up. The ditch soldiers laughed. At last the German artillery, so devastatingly accurate, had connected with the right target. At last one bunch, at least, of Army people was learning the hard way to stay in the rear and to leave the fighting to the people who knew about such things, the non-Army.

For anyone more deeply interested, the only military sociologist of any stature, Bill Mauldin, studied the same problem in the same laboratory, reached similar conclusions and has laid them out in considerable detail in his Complete Works, 1942–45.

The Army, as it grows ever less capable in its proper field of fighting wars, grows ever more supple and adaptable in the once foreign field of forensics. As it loses battle after battle to opponents hopelessly outclassed by its big guns and big planes and big ships off the coast, it gets better and better at turning words and ideas to its own account. It may have reached its peak in this line in turning back the congressional attempt to put an end to the draft.

The occasion was obviously a difficult one for old Army men, for part of the package designed to end the draft was a big increase for all hands. To oppose the bill it was necessary for Army men to oppose pay increases for themselves. But, to their credit, they bit the bullet, cried, Lawd, No, Brer Fox, we don't want no pay raises, and did in the end of the draft. The big argument advanced was astonishing: the draft should be continued, it was argued, lest an all-professional Army feel cut off, "alienated," from the rest of the country and perhaps one day make a play for power, in the way of armies in less fortunate countries all over the world.

The argument was persuasive and the draft was continued. But the argument was perhaps just a shade too clever. For the fact is that we have had a professional, alienated Army for as long as we have had an Army at all. The professionals are called the officer corps and the Army may well be right in its argument against ending the draft. It may well be that professional soldiers are alienated from the country's values, especially the general officers.

If so, fortunately a remedy is at hand, suggested, or at least implied, by the argument strenuously put forward in defense of the draft. If the draft is good for the citizenry at large, it is even better for the officer caste and especially for the general officer caste, whose members the rest of us have thoughtlessly allowed to take up our burdens, to get alienated, to feel suspicious of democratic developments and to become grist for the reactionary-revolutionary mill. It is, after all, officers and especially generals who have pulled off most of the military coups with which the world has been burdened from ancient Rome to modern Greece. The possibility can be circumvented by the simple expedient of drafting our colonels and our joint chiefs of staff the same way we now draft our privates and corporals.

Top and middle management personnel drafted in

from General Electric and U.S. Steel would certainly feel no compulsion to sacrifice the war for the sake of the Army and, granted that—who knows?—they might even start winning again.

The Unfree Nonenterprisers

God knows—and so do men—there is every justification for the American doctrine and policy of the separation of Church and State. The evils of the state church in Europe are manifest in phenomena as different from one another as the Holy Inquisition, the Thirty Years' War, and the Archdeacons and Rural Deans of Anthony Trollope's novels.

But the brilliant stroke of Jefferson and the rest that put established churches out of the purview of the American government has not been an entirely unmixed blessing. Whether because nature abhors a vacuum, or because man cannot rest until he molds some mud into a shape he can call his god, or for some other reason, the American Republic, once it declared against an established American Church, has reeled from one surrogate state religion to another, some good, some bad, most mixed, and all of them against the clear intent of Jefferson's brilliant stroke.

At various times we have fancied ourselves a nation of worshipers of States' Rights, Free Silver, Prohibition, Free Thought, Free Speech, The Open Range, The Closed Homestead, The Public School and Universal Sufferage. Perhaps it says something about the nature of the American society that every one of these ersatz religions is clearly a tool, a means to some other end elevated to the lofty religious status of being an end to itself.

But by all odds, the strangest device we have ever 'blazoned on our banners is that of Free Enterprise.

Free Enterprise is a way of making change, a way of directing traffic, a way of keeping accounts, and a way of producing and distributing the necessities and luxuries of life throughout a society. It is variously like a conveyor belt or a railroad train, a game of dice or a horse race. At its best it is a system of mechanics. As a system —more accurately, a spirit—of production and distribution, it worked reasonably well from the eighteenth century, when it was invented, through the end of the nineteenth century, when it faltered and began to die.

What a thing to have for a religion!

It is superfluous to add that it only became a religion when it was almost dead, early in the present century. This is common enough among mankind's cult objects.

The virtues of sports in our colleges and universities, for example, only became a matter of belief when collegiate sport itself had been transformed into a branch of professional athletics. Likewise, Americans only became enamored of the values of small-town life when the small town had become an anachronism. When it was actually an existing way of life for the majority of Americans, that majority couldn't wait to shake its dust from their feet.

Not only is Free Enterprise a rather sleazy cult object at best—rather like belonging to the First Church of Christ, Stockbroker or to the Evangelical Brotherhood of Latter Day Wholesalers—but since its adoption as a state religion, and even before that, it has had any number of very bad effects on our society.

In the nineteenth century, although the creed had not yet been formulated as such, it was a style of economic life. Trapped by that style, we allowed a perfectly good and useful system of cheap water transport, the canals, to silt up, lie unfinished, and largely perish, simply because the entreprenurial edge of economic adventure had moved on to the railroads. In our own century, with the creed thoroughly established, we have allowed rail transport to slip steadily, mile by mile of track, into the past and into disuse, simply because entrepreneurial fashion—by now heavily dosed with state capitalism in the form of direct subsidies and tax benefits—has pushed on to air and highway travel.

In the professions and the arts, which ought to be above the marketplace, the anachronistic creed of Free Enterprise has had results at least as deleterious as it has in transportation. In England, equipped with a state religion, a Harley Street physician would have always taken umbrage at the notion that he was in any way connected with trade, that his practice of the healing arts was the same as being a greengrocer or an ironmonger. In America, making do with the jerry-built state religion of Free Enterprise, our doctors have for years been duped into thinking themselves tradesmen, and therefore into fighting most unflatteringly against all efforts to restrict the fruits of trade by insuring citizens adequate medical care.

Our lawyers, likewise downgraded into tradesmen in the name of Free Enterprise, have on occasion opposed the humanization of divorce laws and automobile insurance procedures chiefly because the reforms would cut into their income. They might as well have been hawking cabbages in the market.

In the arts, in spite of recent, very hesitant steps in the direction of the universal practice of civilization, the United States remains the single nation in the world today, and apparently in all of history as well, that does not, as a matter of course, subsidize all the arts very heavily. The reason is not that we are uncultured boors compared to all other peoples—look at the Germans—but simply that, gulled by our would-be state religion of Free Enterprise, we have taken it for granted that if the arts were worth their existence, they would automatically support themselves at the box office. If they did not support themselves, they weren't worthy of existence—and so long, Shakespeare.

Yet, while we have been very willing to apply the

strict Free Enterprise Laws of Supply and Demand and the Invisible Hand and all that falderal to such peripheral areas as opera houses and poor people trying to con their way into expensive surgery, in the very heart of our economic society, in big-time production and distribution, our Free Entrepreneurs have been fairly fast and loose with the rules of the game. They complain regularly about the application of the Antitrust Laws, but of course the Antitrust Laws and the laws against conspiracy in restraint of trade are the only things that have preserved, like loving antiquarians, what remnants of Free Enterprise we still have in this country. Free Enterprise is always said to be in danger from Creeping Socialism as well as from Rampant Communism, but its greatest blows in this country have come from the hands of the Free Enterprisers themselves. They do it in every time they get the chance.

An illustration. For years and years and years, the principal preacher in praise of Free Enterprise in this country was a man named Ralph Cordiner, head of General Electric. He was a kind of one-man *Reader's Digest* in constant defense of the American Way of Life, which, he assured his audiences and readers, was just another name for the Free Enterprise System.

Then, shockingly, a small crowd of General Electric executives were held up by the law for antitrust violations and for conspiring in restraint of trade.

They were convicted handily, the evidence being overwhelmingly against them. The case involved General Electric and its principal competitors. The executives had gotten together to circumvent government procedures for competitive bidding. The idea, of course, is for the government to publish its specifications for a project, for interested and competent parties to figure how they can profitably meet the specifications and make a profit. The parties then submit bids and the low man wins. This style of secret bidding is a classic form of Free Enterprise, with each competitor on his own and the Invisible Hand awarding the prize to the most efficient, ingenious and diligent, just like it says in *The Wealth of Nations*.

That wasn't good enough for General Electric and it wasn't good enough for the firm's competitors. Instead of following the prescribed procedures, the executives of the supposedly competing firms got together ahead of time, agreed among themselves on whose turn it was to be low bidder, and then submitted bids calculated to give the award to the firm selected by themselves. The winning bids were handed around strictly on the basis of the size of the firm, and there were elaborate codes both among the so-called competitors and within the ranks at General Electric, the latter code consisting largely of broad winks and grimaces as one executive explained to another how devoted the old firm was to the principles of Free Enterprise and secret bidding.

There were trials. There were convictions. Some of the felons went to jail for no great period and fines were levied against the felonious firms. Thereupon the Justice Department, then led by Attorney General Nicholas DeB. Katzenbach, in one of those administrative decisions that regularly subvert the Congress and the courts, gave General Electric the privilege of deducting its triple damages fines from its taxable income. The principle seemed to be that the costs of crime should be deductible business expenses for the criminals. The whole adventure cost General Electric next to nothing. The conspirators were in effect invited to try the game again, perhaps to keep the Justice Department's Antitrust Division in practice.

Throughout all the unpleasantness, Mr. Cordiner, apostle of the Free Enterprise so rudely violated by his henchmen, presented himself, in public testimony and in private assurances, as fool rather than knave. He pretty well had to be one or the other and he cheerfully testified that he hadn't a clue as to what was going on in his company.

The incident is a paradigm, a scale model, of the role of Free Enterprise as the state religion for which we fight the wicked Communists wherever they appear—although we seem to have some predeliction for fighting them when they appear in small countries just emerging from colonial rule.

The first great body blows to Free Enterprise as an actual working market system were delivered by such nineteenth-century rascals as John D. Rockefeller and Commodore Vanderbilt. Permanently crippled by those blows, the system staggered on through the twentieth century to receive more punishment at the hands of General Electric and its friendly competitors. Dangerously weakened by the betrayals of its alleged friends, Free Enterprise is now receiving its death blows from the Department of Defense. Like Mr. Cordiner, the war preparation efforts of this country is dedicated to the defense of Free Enterprise even as its practices viciously undermine whatever is left of the grand old marketing system.

The Defense Department's system for scuttling Free Enterprise is as beautiful in its simplicity as that of Mr. Cordiner's subordinates for sabotaging competitive bidding. In some ways it is even simpler and therefore more beautiful. While the electrical engineers of consent felt constrained to go through the motions of operating in a free market, albeit with many a wink, nod and nudge in the ribs, the Pentagon's defenders of Free Enterprise sink the principle without even a formal obeisance. Contracts are, as they say, negotiated directly, which means no competitive bidding at all, even phony.

Moreover, contracts are increasingly negotiated with firms that have come into existence solely to win and to execute contracts from the Defense Department, with the principal asset often being an ex-officer who has the personal connections to land the contract that puts the outfit in business.

Moreover even than that, of course, despite occasional fluctuations downward due to approaching elections and the need to look economy-minded on the part of the President and his Secretary of Defense, despite such seasonal downdrafts, the trend in Defense spending has been up, up, up, for a quarter of a century now, not only in absolute terms but in percentages of the nations's budget, which in turn has been growing steadily every year for Democrats and Republicans alike.

What all these moreovers add up to is that every day in every way the Department of Defense and its civilian contractors are whacking away at the system of Free Enterprise they are all so dedicated to defending.

According to Mr. Cordiner and other evangelists of

freedom, any substantial economic system that isn't Free Enterprise has to be Socialism. The Defense bonanza being very substantial and certainly not Free Enterprise, it qualifies as Socialism. It is mildly surprising that the vigilante groups around the country who see the red hand of Socialism in efforts to help sick people afford the medical care they need, or in feeble attempts to help Negroes into full citizenship, have been totally blind to the biggest triumph of Creeping Socialism yet, its all but complete takeover of military procurement. In the language of the witch-hunters of yore—who may not be quite as yore as we like to think—these things don't just happen. Somebody makes them happen and that somebody is a Moscow agent. The question is, which of the joint chiefs is a Commie? Or, How many? Reverend MacIntyre, a nation betrayed may ask, where were you when the Pentagon went Red?

According to the same evangelists, the principal distinguishing note of Socialism is that it doesn't work. The Russians, for instance, are only now beginning to create the traffic jams and air pollution we in the capitalist West have enjoyed for two generations. The Chinese think they can make steel mills in every peasant's backyard. That sort of thing.

By that standard, the Pentagonians are super-Socialists. There are times when everything they touch seems to fall apart in their hands.

They have spent millions on airplanes for South Vietnam and forgotten to insulate the electrical wiring against the considerable heat encountered in that country. On arrival, the wires melted and the planes were useless.

Their most classic bit of Socialist incompetence was

the time they launched a submarine and forgot to close the seacocks. The brand-new, ultra-expensive ship went down the ways and kept on going, down to the bottom of the sea, lacking only Buster Keaton on the bridge.

Their most improbable achievement in this line was the dropping of a small submarine from a Navy helicopter on a golf course in Virginia Beach, not only demolishing the vessel, but even missing the water trap. Not unexpectedly, Navy spokesmen replied to all queries that what the submarine was doing up there with the helicopter was classified information.

In general there are two results of the noncompetitive, no-bidding process whereby military contracts are bestowed by the Pentagon. First, the damn stuff doesn't work when and if it is delivered. And second whether it works or not, it always costs from half again as much to three or four hundred percent as much as originally scheduled. The factor of nonperformance on delivered goods has become so scandalous that even Congress, —which is usually pretty tolerant of nonperformance, out of common decency—became aroused. It badgered Secretary Laird into adoping "Fly Before You Buy" as a procurement slogan, but whether it's anything more than a slogan remains to be seen.

As to the cost overruns, as they are delicately called, there is little anyone can do until the whole system is broken up and there seems to be no way to break up the system.

The system has grown out of the enormous increase in retired military officers in recent years and is not unlike the serious problem of the enormous increase in Ph.D.'s due to draft deferments once thoughtlessly granted for graduate studies. In the old days the normal retired military officer wrote his memoirs, or taught at a military school, went hunting and fishing, or sat around the Army-Navy Club harumphing at the day's headlines.

The population explosion at the Pentagon has altered that balance of nature drastically. The Army-Navy Club, even with eight floors, can't begin to offer chairs to all the retired Pentagonians, just as the American university establishment can't begin to employ all the Ph.D.'s.

On the whole, the Army has provided for its excess retired personnel better than the university has for its excess holders of high degrees. It moves them into defense industries. As procurement officers reach retirement age they naturally and easily move to the other side of the table. They go to work for the people they used to hire, which is an interesting experiment in role reversal that has to have its effects in advance on future employees. At the same time, they begin to sell to the people who used to work for them, their military assistants who have now moved up into the jobs formerly occupied by the new salesmen. The new procurement officers cannot but reflect that soon they, too, will be out there looking for a job and selling hardware to the old firm at the Pentagon.

Is it possible that personal considerations of one's past and future affect the participants in these negotiations at every step of the way? Is it conceivable that such considerations have something to do with the shoddy quality of the work delivered to the Pentagon and the amazing escalation of prices?

It is possible. It is conceivable. Especially if the only

other feasible explanation of such a dunderheaded performance as the Pentagon has been turning in is the hypothesis that the whole place has become one vast cell in the secret Communist network set up by Trotsky, a military man, to subvert and suborn the defenders of Free Enterprise.

The United States has trouble enough being a Republic, let alone a participatory democracy, but still, in clumsy fashion, it does manage to conduct many of its affairs in terms of some sort of representation of the people. This representation is formalized through the Congress. It would be a strange thing indeed if a system of Socialist disbursement of federal funds as vast as the one the Pentagon has built and presided over were carried on without collaboration from the legislative branch of the government. Both houses of Congress worry about the defense of the United States; both houses worry about the spending of federal funds. Both houses have taken part in the El Dorado the Pentagon has found in noncompetitive, no-bidding contract-letting. The system would be unthinkable without full participation by Congress. It would be militarism. As things are, the same system is representative government. But as on Animal Farm, some representatives are more representative than other representatives.

As a general rule, the most representative of all are those from the South. When the Southern Armies were disarmed following the surrender at Appomattox, it was a grave humiliation for the gallant cavaliers and slaveholders of the Old Confederacy, but they have had their revenge. Gradually they have taken over, by way of recompense, the entire Union Army, and the Union Army these days is big money. They have accomplished this through the normal procedures of representative government, especially the government of Representative Mendel Rivers, late Chairman of the Military Affairs Committee, and his magic formula for defending Free Enterprise by draining Yankee dollars into his native South Carolina by way of the Socialist defense contracts of the Pentagon.

Ideologically improbable as the formula is, it lies behind the fastest growth in American industry since the ball-point pen.

Way Down South

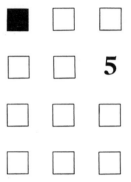

5

Vice President Agnew, by way of prepping up for his 1970 campaign to unseat the dread Radic-Libs in Congress, addressed a dinner given in honor of Representative Rivers by his clients and beneficiaries in the Pentagon and in defense industry. The Vice President, with the rhetorical mastery that has made his name a household word, constructed his speech on the conceit that the man they meant to honor had offered his congressional district, Charleston, South Carolina, as a sacrifice to the welfare of the nation by accepting the burden of elaborate military and naval installations and manufacturing projects.

Down the list went the noted comedian, enumerating camps and forts and special forces, shipbuilding, military supplies of all kinds, barrels of federal money rolling down to Charleston, and the kindly, white-haired, old bon vivant generously giving it all a home in the salubrious clime and historic locale of his district and his state.

It was quite a speech, perhaps the most daring act of political *hubris* since *Life* magazine swore in Thomas E. Dewey as President a week before the election of 1948. It was notable as the most succinct statement of how the military-industrial complex actually works. It was notable because no one in the audience, not the manufacturers' agents who had got the thing up, not the Pentagonians who graced it with their spiffy dress blues, certainly not the slyly chuckling guest of honor, evinced the slightest idea that there was anything even mildly embarrassing in the recital. And, of course, it was notable because the place was not struck by lightning before Agnew had finished reeling off the roll of ravenous rapacity and listing the loot of the long-lasting legislator.

The military-industrial complex is not the two-way street that Eisenhower's name for it implies. It is a three-way equilateral triangle, with Congress providing the third angle. It is also part of the Southern Revenge on the rest of the country, as the Vice President implied but did not quite spell out.

The arrangement has come about by a series of accidents in the national legislature and in world affairs, none of which was engineered by the South; but accidental or not, there is a certain appropriateness about the South's finally making it big with arms.

That profession is predominantly a Southern folkway in this country. The South, as you can learn at any Jefferson Davis Annual Birthday Ball, was settled by Laughing Cavaliers, and Laughing Cavaliers, when they aren't laughing, are practicing at arms. Building upon that natural inclination, the Southerners became big farmers but their agriculture was tenant agriculture and then slave agriculture, both of which are distinguished by having most of the work done by people other than the farmer, who naturally turns to arms and war to fill his idle hours. This is also the way it worked throughout the Dark and Middle Ages in Europe and in such places as Prussia right up to the twentieth century. It worked that way in the South to such effect that by the Civil War the majority of higher-ranking officers owed allegiance to the South. Had war still been primarily a matter of military intelligence, the North would have been beaten long before the genius of Grant was fully formed and given its necessary scope. But even as the emerging town engaged and finally defeated the big farmer-soldier of the Middle Ages, so the North was forging something new under the sun, heavy industry, and used it to inflict damage upon the South such as had not been seen since the Thirty Years' War.

After Appomattox, the South remained in arms. The profession now also served the purpose it had long served in England of providing jobs for younger sons. In a sense, all the Southern sons in the postwar years were disinherited younger sons and therefore they became soldiers. As in the years before the Civil War, Southerners moved naturally into and up through the ranks of the American armed forces in numbers disproportionate to the size of the region in the country as a whole.

There was, in this Southern return to arms, no particular thought of using arms to reverse the results of the Civil War. That was accomplished by other means, chiefly political.

At home, terrorism and the raising of the Democratic Party to religious status effectively deprived the Southern Negro of his newly attained status as a citizen and voter. After the brief intoxication of the Reconstruction, the Negro again became a slave, this time without the benefits of slavery that we can learn about at those same Jefferson Davis jamborees. After 1880 the Negro didn't vote, he didn't learn to read in his schools, and he didn't learn the trades, let alone the professions. He remained the crude labor he had been under slavery but he no longer had the small comfort of the economic security provided on the old plantation.

In the Southernized armed forces, he was, naturally, the happy, smiling, all-the-time-singing mess boy in the Navy and the shiftless, shuffling mule-skinner in the Army. If there was any real doubt about who won the Civil War, it was only necessary to examine the position of the Negro in Southern and American military society from 1880 to 1960.

If the South reimposed slavery on the Negro, which it did, it took a different course with the other Civil War question, that of secession or union. The tradition of secession went back well before the Civil War to Congressman Rivers' great fellow South Carolinian, Calhoun, in the 1830s. The War Between the States did end

Carolina's secessionist leanings, but these were replaced not by the simple giving in and becoming a member of the Union like the other states, but by the new move to dominate the Union that refused to be dissolved.

The domination has been spotty but it has been effective in certain areas. Early in the twentieth century the South achieved its major breakthrough in national domination when both houses of Congress adopted seniority as their governing principle. The idea was to curb the chaos of the party caucus and the tyranny of the party leaders by providing a sensible, orderly progression to power within the committees and the houses as a whole. The result has been the enshrining of mediocrity as our principal legislative virtue, especially Southern mediocrity.

The region that gave the country Washington, Jefferson, Jackson and Calhoun, now sends to Congress, as statesmen of great national power, the likes of Russell Long, Strom Thurmond, John McMillan, James Eastland and Byrd Junior. The reason for the striking drop in quality is essentially the same reason the Pentagon's favored few no-bid contractors have such difficulty making an airplane that will stay up in the air or a rifle that will keep on shooting: no competition. Once the conquered rebels were readmitted to voting rights, they moved en masse into the Democratic Party on the grounds that Lincoln was a Republican. By and large they have stayed there ever since, giving the South an effective veto power over the Democrats and also ensuring that once a Southern Democratic politician managed to land a seat in Congress, he was there for life for all the competition he'd get from Republicans.

That same turn of political events gave the South working control of the machinery of both houses of Congress. Once the Senate and the House of Representatives decided to let themselves be governed by their own gerontocracy, the legislative branch of the national government automatically became Southern-ruled and has remained that way throughout the present century. Newly enfranchised Negroes and the growth of Republican suburbs in the South may or may not be changing the picture, but in the national government, the South still retains vast power, accumulated through the sheer ability of its legislators to stay in office once elected.

Over the years the power was used with relative restraint compared to the way it could have been used. As senior partners in the New Deal, the South naturally has made a good thing out of Roosevelt's farm legislation. Senator Eastland of Mississippi alone annually draws two or three hundred thousand dollars on the basis of this program, which to this day subsidizes the growth of cancer in American throats and lungs through its support of tobacco farming, and the dislocation of rural Negroes through its subsidization of mechanized agriculture in the South.

Perhaps the principal token of Southern dominance of the national government was its dominance of the national capital, Washington, which it ruled through the respective committees on the affairs of the District of Columbia. Segregation, for instance, was rigidly enforced in the schools and theaters of the city from which Lincoln directed the war against slavery. The harrowing of the District of Columbia seems to have been a point of pride with some Southern members, who, at election time, went back home to recite for constituent approval how the Washington Negroes were being kept in their place by the Southern Congress.

Following the victories of civil rights legislation in the 1960s, it has seemed to residents of the capital that the main way Congress exacts its tribute is in transportation. It has steadfastly refused to build public parking facilities, such as are familiar in most American cities of the motor age; instead, real estate operators provide high-priced parking on lots they are holding until enough are assembled to put up a new building. Congress likewise has been generally antisubway, presumably since the underground system would be of benefit chiefly to Negroes. On the other hand, liquor prices have been kept low, although the District of Columbia could dearly use the income most jurisdictions derive from that source, and by congressional fiat, taxi prices are among the lowest in the country.

The picture that emerges from all this is of the Southern Committee Chairman who drives to the Capitol, where he has free parking, and takes cheap taxis the rest of the day, drinking cheap booze as he rolls along, all the time thinking up new ways to impress upon the nation's capital that whatever the results at Gettysburg, Vicksburg and the March through Georgia, the South has now, decisively, won the War Between the States, and don't you forget it.

But all of this put together didn't amount to so much. New England shipowners did better in their time at the federal pay window. Oil men from the first Rockefeller to H. L. Hunt have done better as individuals on government handouts than the South had done as a region— until very recently.

But in the very recent past things began to happen. The Southern control of congressional machinery and the Southern affinity for the profession of arms were both long established before the big break. They were like modest family investments, all but forgotten though their regular dividends were appreciated, often making the difference between genteel poverty and moderate affluence. In World Wars I and II and in the programs since, the South reaped a small harvest through bilking Northern servicemen sent south for training in the countryside. Camps, posts and forts were built and kept in business. Then, in the years after the second great war of the century, the bonanza struck. It was as if the companies that had been paying those modest dividends suddenly discovered the office buildings were erected on the biggest gold mine of all time.

They were. It was the International Communist Nuclear Missile Gold Mine and the principal entrances, through Congress and through the Pentagon, all turned out to be way down South in Dixie.

Such is the elaborate and at times somewhat fortuitous history that built up to the grand climax of Spiro Agnew reading the golden legend of big items from the federal fisc brought home by Mendel Rivers like captives chained to his chariot.

The South was not alone in the miraculous rain of pennies from heaven. In the new, scientific warfare, brains were needed of a technological kind more often found outside the South than in it. Massachusetts and Connecticut came in not only because of the technical brains to be found in residence along Highway 128 circling Boston, but also, assuredly, because of all those Kennedys in the early 1960s and because of the practically Southern endurance of Speaker McCormack, who came, when you think of it, from South Boston. California came in both because of its technical brains and its existing related industries, but also because of the concurrence of nationally important Republican figures from the state at a crucial moment. In some ways even more preposterous than the rise of the South generally as the chief beneficiary of the imminence of Armageddon was the emergence of Texas as a center for scientific-technological skills based almost solely on the manipulative skills of Senate Majority Leader Lyndon Johnson and House Speaker Sam Rayburn.

There is a lot to be said for the South. It is a much-maligned and mistreated part of the country, as it never tires of pointing out. As to slavery, the South, after all, came into the Union, the new country, with that peculiar institution already in existence. It wasn't something the South tried to sneak in on the other states. Except for Negroes, white Southerners have suffered more from slavery and from its abolition than any other national group; and while some belated efforts are at least being made to compensate Negroes for the deprivations endured by them and by their ancestors, no one has yet suggested so much as a reeducation program for white Southerners, who need some such device no less acutely.

As to the military connection, it has been on balance, an honorable one and one of great service to the country as a whole. The South took over the military largely for the same reason it took over the national legislature: there wasn't enough profit in either one to attract the high rollers from the North and the West. Without much help from the high rollers, Southern arms leadership gave America the nucleus needed for the two great wars of the century. If you believe that Hitler was a criminal maniac who absolutely had to be stopped, you could make a case that the American South was one of the big things that did stop him.

If you take a more fashionable view of the wars we have fought since the post-Civil War Southern military ascendency, you still cannot fault the South for what you object to. We may indeed have carved out our position as hemispheric moderator to save United Fruit's balance sheet. We may have fought the Kaiser to turn back the awful threat of analine dyes from German chemical works. We may even have atomized Hiroshima to prevent Asiatic trade from falling into the hands of the Asiatics. If all these things were true, it is also true that the benefits accrued chiefly to men in the North and the West, while the military leadership needed to secure those benefits came from the South.

The South's pattern of reversing the verdict of the battlefield and winning the war a couple of decades after it was over has since been copied by Germany and Japan with no payment of royalties and with incomparably greater economic benefits than the poor South has ever enjoyed from its capture of the American Congress. For years, assorted Southern crackpots assured their hearers that the South would one day be compensated for the loss of the property in human bodies, the slaves who were freed. For years the suggestion struck most humane ears as absurd and slightly obscene. But since then the American government has decided that the family Krupp had to be compensated for essentially the same loss—the slaves lost to the cannon factory when the Allies won. So there may be a case for the South, too.

But if there is, it is time and past time the case was handled directly, for what it is. What it comes down to, basically, is that the rest of the country owes some sort of debt to the South for having defeated the South in battle. It is exactly the sort of debt we acknowledge in respect to Germany and Japan and perhaps the time has come to do so for the South. But such direct payment will be infinitely less expensive and harmful in other ways than the indirect methods we have adopted through the industrial-military-Southern-Congressmen complex.

What we probably ought to do is to pass a law to the effect that any member of Congress from the states of the Old Confederacy, on achieving his, say, twentieth year in Congress, is thereafter entitled to free airplane rides wherever he wants to go, to substantial federal investment in the industry of his home town, to periodic honorific banquets, and to a lifetime supply of sippin' whiskey deliverable on demand. The system would be costly, of course, but it would be miniscule in cost compared to the elaborate machinery of war materiel and personnel we now support for, in great part, the same purposes.

The alternative would be congressional reform, with advancement based on merit and energy, but there isn't a chance of that as long as the South remains in control of Congress.

The Nonprofit Empire

6

Imperialists, the Soviets call us regularly, but we dismiss the charge with ease. It's part of their Newspeak, the special Communist language in which, as in Humpty-Dumpty's, words mean what you want them to mean. But perhaps we dismiss the charge too easily. We may, after all, be an empire without entirely realizing it. In spite of the inscription and the painting to match over a grand staircase in the U.S. Capitol, "Westward the Course of Empire Takes Its Way," we have never really believed it, interpreting "Empire" in that instance in some sort of mystical way—the spirit of progress, or of mankind, or of history—rather than as something on the order of Rudyard Kipling holding dominion over palm and pine.

But empire always has had its mystical side, as the Russians know better than anyone. In the Western World, which is the one we're stuck with whether we like it or not, the idea of empire begins with the Romans. Alexander's empire doesn't really count: it outlasted him by only a decade and seems to have been created in a fit of boyish enthusiasm; the way other boys collect stamps, he collected kingdoms. The Romans were different. Their empire was a serious effort to organize the world and it had a good long run, lasting in legal form right up to the beginning of the nineteenth century and in spirit considerably beyond that, possibly even until today.

The Roman Empire has never been repeated successfully, but Europe has constantly remembered the idea behind it. The continent revived the idea in the Carolingian kings, in the Ottonians and finally in the Hapsburgs. Napoleon was not kidding when he called himself emperor; he was reviving the ancient dream of European unity and embodying it in his person. Hitler, of course, did the same without the title. Since the end of World War II, the mystical idea of the Roman Empire and of European unity has been bodied forth in the daily dull shopkeepers' association that is the Common Market: when the ambassadors meet to arrange an exchange of onions, Charlemagne stirs in his grave.

The Romans were so extremely fecund in these matters that they created not one empire but two; the Western, which has wound its way down through popes and adventurers to the accountants meeting in Brussels; and also the Eastern, which has had just as curious a history and is at least as much alive. The history begins with the Emperor Diocletian, one of the most extraordinary political thinkers ever to exercise political power. To solve complicated problems of administrative convenience, political succession and military viability, Diocletian boldly split the empire he had inherited by arms, much as Alexander had cut the Gordian knot, with a single stroke. The Eastern, or Byzantine, Empire, its capital at Constantinople, survived and flourished for a thousand years after the Western Empire fell to the barbarians and became a troubling memory in Europe. The Eastern Empire did fall, however, to the invading Turks who still hold the capital and once held all that part of the world.

At that point a strange shift occurred. The Russians, of all people, discovered that they were the true heirs of the Roman Empire. The formula was that Rome was the first Rome, Byzantium the second Rome and Moscow the third Rome. That idea stayed alive throughout the rise and fall of the Czarist Empire and is undoubtedly alive yet. Mingled with nineteenth-century pan-Slavism, the idea of the third and final Roman Empire is expressed— along with obvious realities of international power politics—in the Russian ascendancy in Eastern Europe, in the border-bickering with China and in the manipulations in the Middle East. Communism has provided Russia with what the poor, decadent old Romanoffs never had, a burning religious faith to make the idea of Moscow as the third Rome dynamic and expansionist, the state annointed by God to bring the true gospel to the heathen beyond the borders.

Aware as we are of this Russian history, and aware, too, of Soviet-determined repression of all independence movements in Eastern Europe, we laugh at Russian charges of American imperialism. Talk about the pot calling the kettle imperialist. Around the turn of the century we may have flirted with the rhetoric of empire, but since then we operate under such international auspices as may be available, the League of Nations, the U.N. or regional treaty groupings. Clearly, it seems to us, the Russians call us imperialists to mask the fact that they themselves have built up an empire in Eastern Europe and show no hesitation about extending it anyplace that looks likely.

That may indeed be part of the Soviet motivation in its name-calling. But they may also be calling us those dirty names because that's the way we look to them. One common note of all empires is the characteristic of having imperial troops stationed in foreign lands. Diocletian was constantly dispatching the legions from one end of the empire to the other to hold it together. The Spanish occupied Mexico and Peru, to say nothing of Sicily and Flanders, when their empire was at its height. The English, of course, flung their thin, red line around the world and kept it in place with British troops from the eighteenth century through the end of World War II. Today the United States has its troops all over the place. American military men turn up in some strength in Iceland and England, Spain and Turkey, Japan and Korea. In some places they are accompanied or led by officials with vice-regal functions if not titles. Especially our troops and our viceroys have been found, in the years since World War II, in West Germany, and in Vietnam and its neighbors. If maintaining troops in foreign lands is a mark of empire, we've got good credentials. That may be what the Russians have in mind.

We have, however, managed to create a decidedly different kind of empire in at least one important respect. Empires have always had their troops all over the territory. They have always believed in some mystique or other of saving the world from barbarism or Marxism. But empires, by and large, have also made money and when they stopped making money they stopped being empires. The Romans organized the world and maintained the peace and exported law along the roads as far as they could reach, but they also shipped back to Rome some portion of everything they could lay their hands on. The bread in the bread-and-circuses formula came with the Egyptian grain ships. In more modern times, while it is undeniably true that the immense benefits of English common law were being conferred on India by the British rule there, it is also true that the tea and the brass went back to the home country. The French brought the enlightenment of the Ecole Normale to selected Arabs, Africans and Southeast Asiatics, but they also shipped back the rubber and the oil in substantial quantities. Thus has it ever been, the Dutch bringing chocolate from Indonesia, the Belgians uranium from the Congo. The values and virtues of metropolitan Europe were freely available for colonial export, but the colonials were expected to put up a little something in exchange, usually the bulk of their national treasure. That was empire in modern times and it ran much of the world through the nineteenth century and part of the twentieth.

We have changed all that. For the first time in history we Americans have invented the nonprofit empire.

The tale is told most briefly by reference to what are obviously the principal seats of our empire, West and East. In Europe, on any scale of measurement, our imperial headquarters is Germany. Since crushing the Nazi threat, we have kept thousands of troops on German soil. In the traditional management of empire, these troops should have been supervising the gathering in of native production and the shipping of it back to the homeland. On the Roman and British models, we should by now be up to our ears in low-cost sauerkraut. Nothing of the sort has happened. On the contrary, conquered Germany has led the race of European recovery, rapidly making itself the wonder child of postwar economy and even threatening the fundamental base of the American economy on its own ground, the superhighway. It took a quarter of a century, but in model-year 1971, the competition of defeated Germany forced the American automobile industry to bring out small, economical, easy-to-repair cars designed chiefly as transportation from place to place, rather than as status symbols or sex surrogates. It is difficult to imagine a more complete conquest of the conqueror by the conquered.

The Germans managed this in a number of ways, but chiefly by getting rid of the awful burden of armaments they had labored under, off and on, since Barbarossa. After enduring all those German gangsters, the West decided the Germans couldn't be trusted with guns, a reasonable enough conclusion. Therefore, German protection was provided by American guns and American gunners. The American people, however, paid the Germans for putting up with their American protection, and the American soldiers, overpaid by German standards, spent big money on everything in Germany. Through these and other channels, American money drained out of America into Germany. Eventually the Germans could even afford to revive an army of their own, with American equipment, but they did it more as an act of ancestral piety than as a move toward providing for their own defense. It just didn't seem right for Germans not to have an army and now they could afford one, having got rich on ours.

On the other side of the world, in Indochina, the same situation came into existence, only worse. Our failure to make money out of our occupation of postwar Germany was, in a sense, understandable, even inevitable. After all, the Germans were our cultural equals. They had the same technical knowledge that we had, the same Wernher von Braun and other scientific marvels. They would naturally know what a conqueror would be up to and be ready to foil the exploitation. But Indochina was quite a different story. Subject to invasions from many directions for many centuries, the Indochinese had been kept in technical innocence by their French masters. They had an immensely rich agricultural country and a valuable rubber industry. They constituted a classic example for imperial exploitation, had indeed been exploited by the French right up to the day of that nation's final withdrawal, and would certainly have been exploited fully by the Japanese had they been able to stick around a little longer. The imperial Americans began arriving in Indochina disguised as technical advisors on weaponry, rather as the original Anglo-Saxon imperialists in India had come in as tea-tasters. In a few years we gave up the advisor cover story and were fighting away like Ronald Colman in Lucknow—but with what different results.

We have poured our sons and our treasure into Indochina for very dubious gains. Our treasure ran up against the ancient and honorable Asiatic system of family-based graft and inflated it to monstrous proportions. Our sons, for their part, have had much the same effect on the equally ancient local trade of prostitution. The British, the French, the Belgians and the Dutch were all careful in their time to keep the technical marvels strictly in the hands of the European conquerors. Our sheer abundance has been such that we have scattered the shreds and shards of a high technical culture all over the countryside of a very primitive one. The regional politicians can undoubtedly rise to the requisite level of technical competence for living, eventually, in the Riviera homes we have been providing the money for, and to live there in happiness. But the country itself can never cope with the technical flow we have maintained there. The example is familiar in the eighteenth-century engravings of Piranesi, the views of Rome in which his contemporary Italians and foreign visitors creep and peep like midgets among the monuments—the aqueducts, arches and temples—of the ancients. Our departure from Vietnam, should such a departure take place, will leave a similar scene behind, with bamboo and palm reclaiming the airstrips, all our electronic monuments sinking into the eternal jungle.

But the point, of course, is that they are *our* monuments, *their* bamboo shoots. The relationship has got turned around somewhere. What is supposed to happen is for the electronic gear to be used by our colonial young men making a career in the harvesting, treating, packing and shipping of the bamboo trees to imperialist America to be used as fast-growing border screens in suburban homes, and exotic decor in decorators' offices.

The relationship is backward, too, in the matter of marijuana. American youths in their drafted thousands have been going over to Vietnam now for years and getting stoned on cheap, powerful pot, native to the area. "Kids" back from "Nam" claim the stuff there is incomparably better than anything to be smuggled in from Jamaica or Mexico—although the product of these countries, in turn, is miles ahead of anything grown in the fields of Iowa or the windowboxes of Greenwich Village. Cold warriors of the determination of Connecticut's Senator Dodd—had up by the Senate for easy traffic between his campaign coffers and his personal pockets—have had a go at pinning the whole Vietnamese disaster on pot. American boys, the argument goes, have gone over there and been seduced by the stuff so that, their normal American invincibility weakened by the fumes of marijuana, they have been pushed around by the frightful little Viet Cong soldiers and outwitted by their big brothers from the North. It's an attractive argument, wrapping up all together the hated Communist enemy abroad and the dread drug pusher of the American campus and slum life. But again, Dodd willing, the argument misses the point of empire. The relationship is backward. It's supposed to be the other way around. The sweated, exploited natives are supposed to be the ones who seek solace in drugs. The robust, imperialist soldiers are supposed to be the ones who recoil in horror at native ways with drugs and go off to the canteen to guzzle their own honest gin-and-it.

All these strange variations on the theme of empire, these astounding evidences of our somehow having got the whole idea backward, may well be due simply to our having got in on the imperial gravy train shortly after train service was discontinued. We were rather like those small investors in the stock market who are forever getting in just as the big money is getting out, except, of course, that our plunge into empire preferred was and is very big money.

The colonial empire business, a distinct variation from the Romano-European Empire either East or West, was essentially a phenomenon of the century and a half from 1800 to 1950. The inside investors made a lot of money on it in that bull period, and without exception they all got out when that period came to its end. The British departed most gracefully, leaving India and Pakistan to fight it out, Canada to make a new flag. The Belgians and the Dutch recognized a bad thing when they saw it and decamped from Indonesia and the Congo in time to allow both lands to collapse into chaos of different kinds, one called civil war, the other called Sukarno. The French, not unexpectedly, clung the most tenaciously to what remnants of *la gloire* they could fantasize out of torturing the Algerians and the Vietnamese, but eventually even the French called it a day, began regrouping the old firm, chiefly in Africa, and admitted that empire was finished.

At that point the Americans got into the empire line. Years ago, when movies were still fairly new, there was a Wheeler-Woolsey extravaganza set on an American Indian reservation out in Arizona or thereabouts. With the economy of means that is now considered old-fashioned, the show opened with a head shot of an American Indian with accompanying title: "The American Indian has no left sideburn. He has no right sideburn. He has no beard. And he doesn't cut his hair." This was followed by a visual cut to establish the location as an Indian reservation and Wheeler and Woolsey as proprietors of a barber shop. That was about the situation in the empire racket when the United States decided to get into it.

It wasn't that there weren't signs aplenty that this was a bad time to take the imperialist road. The French and their fellow Continentals are beyond our understanding in any circumstances, but the English are our cousins and they were giving the clearest signs of all that the empire at last was sinking beneath the sun. The big sign, which came as rather a cultural shock to most Americans, was the British electorate's giving the heave-ho to Winston Churchill before the war was properly over at all. Old blood-sweat-and-tears had said, among so many other more distinguished observations, that he had not become his majesty's first minister to preside over the dissolution of the British Empire. Whereupon, the first chance they got, the voters turned him out and put in someone who could preside over just that dissolution. That should have been a clue, but we missed it: we blamed the debacle on the cheap desire of the British working class for free dentures and hairpieces; we forgot that the real imperialists in Britain, people of Churchill's class, had been getting free dentures and then some out of empire for a century and more, and, of course, we had no way to foresee that in less than a generation we ourselves would be shopping for socialized bandaids on the cheap.

There was another clue. The Jews. Every empire you can think of in the West has, at one time or another, amused itself by defrauding or murdering the Jews in various numbers. The tradition goes back to Babylon and comes all the way up to Russia with its czarist pogroms and Soviet captivity, to France with Dreyfus and all that, and to Britain with the Jewish Homeland in Palestine. Doing in the Jews has been one of the standard privileges of having an empire, as you may learn from the Arch of Titus in Rome and the Belsen and Buchenwald memorials in Germany. It is a long tradition and Britain was merely carrying it on when, before, during and after World War I, the grand old empire flummoxed the Jews in the matter of the Balfour Declaration. The Homeland would be forthcoming, but don't wait up for it, was the message that gradually became clear to Zionists in Britain and the Middle East. Then, abruptly, with the end of World War II, a change in the pattern appeared. The same old talk about a Homeland in the sweet by-and-by was made, but the Jews weren't being flummoxed anymore. They said thank you very much and they took the Homeland by arms, without waiting any longer for it to be passed around. The point is not the justice of the Jewish cause, nor even the long, long patience of the Jewish people, but simply the evidence of the end of empire that leaps out from the fact of successful Jewish resistance to traditional imperial flimflammery. If empire can no longer suppress the Jews, empire is finished. You could even, if you were mystically inclined, work out scriptural-historical support for the proposition that the Jews are a kind of touchstone of empire: to build an empire is to persecute, defraud, murder or otherwise trammel the Jews. When the Jews strike back and hold empire at bay, empire has reached the end of its run. Since 1948 and even a couple of years before the war of that name, the Jews have fought off the British Empire, the Arab Empire and the Russian Communist Empire, and the Jews survive. This is about as clear a sign as one could want that empire is, to say the least, in long-term eclipse. It's a good time to put your money in something else. But precisely at that moment, the Americans got into empire, posting troops around the globe, entering into imperial alliances and losing money on every imperial ploy that used to be a sure thing.

Why?

It's hard to say, of course, or, from another point of view, it is all too easy to say. Plain old dumbness should never be dismissed without careful examination as the possible root reason behind human actions that seem dumb. It may be that they seem dumb because they *are* dumb, and that's all there is to the mystery. But as an explanation, dumbness has the considerable disadvantage of not being very long. Any loyal American would certainly hope that the explanation for the remarkably stupid timing of his country's entry into imperialism would have more of an explanation than those simple words. Fortunately there are at hand several other explanations, all of them gratifyingly longer.

From a Marxist point of view, any capitalist country has to progress into imperialism just from the nature of the two things, without regard to the historical time at which the transition takes place. The old express train of history keeps puffing along, and when it comes to the switch it takes the turn regardless of whether floods, avalanches and earthquakes have happened since Marx wrote the original schedule. This essentially predestinarian explanation is a little too Calvinistic for most of us, but it does suggest another variant, or even two, of our Calvinist heritage which may well be applicable to our belated imperial dalliance.

One is the late capitalist, and hence late, late Calvinist, economic development known as planned obsolescence. There are two basic interpretations of planned obsolescence, one optimistic and generally put out by the people who practice it, the other pessimistic and adhered to by the people who suffer from that theory of production. The optimistic view is that every day in every way our industrial production gets better and better and therefore the consumer who purchased, say, a super-eight dodecahedron special last year will naturally want to trade it in for a superduper model this year. The process releases last year's model back to the market, making work for used-car salesmen and allowing citizens a rung or two down the ladder to taste of last year's luxe. The pessimistic version, on the other hand, has it that American industry is run by a bunch of planning obsoleters whose job it is to design things so that they will fall apart the day after the warranty expires and thus maintain a lively demand for replacements. Either way, obviously, the thing about planned obsolescence is the steady discarding of produced goods by consumers who, just a few decades ago, would have been in the market for goods likely to last a lifetime. It is more than conceivable that if planned obsolescence in either sense has become a fundamental strain in our economy, then empire, and the constant war that it entails when entered into prematurely or post-maturely, are the inevitable best natural obsoleters any planner can ask. If you obsolete a motor car by changing the design from bulbous swellings to bauhaus sleekness, or kitchen appliances by changing the fashionable color from avocado to desert sand, there will always be the cheapies in the crowd who will struggle along with last year's shape or tint and there's nothing you can do about it. But when you obsolete something with a cannon or a bomber, it stays obsolete.

The other Calvinist strain operating in favor of our tardy imperialism should be more recognizable, for it is the American Puritan heritage. The stern and rockbound souls who settled in New England in the seventeenth century have left their mark upon our present situation no less than the Laughing Cavaliers whose would-be descendants keep laughing all the way to the bank in Charleston, South Carolina. In a country as big as this one, there has always been the temptation to empire, hence that picture in the Capitol, complete with inscription. But in the United States, thanks to our Puritan heritage and in sharp contrast to the style in other lands, the temptation has always been recognized as a temptation and never confused with opportunity.

At the very beginning of the Puritan residence here, by way of example, the New Englanders discovered that their land was full of rocks. Instead of anticipating the example of later Americans and moving on out to Iowa or some other reservoir of rich soil and easy plowing, the New England Puritan hacked away at his rocky fields in the belief that the added labor was good for his soul.

A somewhat later generation of New England Puritans got into the slave trade, but the manner of this involvement is most instructive. They didn't actually own slaves, not because that was immoral in itself, but because it led to easy living and that was immoral. Owning slaves led to dancing at the cotillion and rocking on the veranda while Uncle Junius fetched up another julep. The Puritan preferred to buy slaves cheap in Africa, sell them dear in Carolina and go home to denounce his customers as wicked slave-owners.

When that record is remembered, it no longer surprises that residually Puritan America only got into the empire trade when the trade had gone to hell completely and was a nonpaying, exceedingly painful, domestically divisive and foreignly fearful line of work. If we'd gone in when the going was good, we might have enjoyed it. Only now, with the bottom dropped out of sight from the market and no recovery in sight, could we become imperialists.

We can't hope to profit from it. It doesn't even offer us the sort of cushioned upbringing a generation or two of Englishmen enjoyed in India and the rest.

We are in it because it is so awful and that's so good for you.

The Paper Condottieri

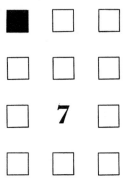

Down in the crypt of the Medici tombs, Michelangelo placed some of his most powerful and expressive sculptures, the Times of Day. The four figures are surmounted by two others, representations of the two exceedingly minor members of the family there interred, Lorenzo and Giuliano de' Medici, not to be confused with their older relatives of the same names, Lorenzo the Magnificent and his murdered brother Giuliano. The two memorial statues together have usually been taken as the Active Life and the Contemplative Life, an interpretation that has troubled some scholars since it would seem to reverse the actual characters of the Medici dukelings. Like all great artists, however, Michelangelo was a prophet and it is only now, in the fullness of time, that his entire meaning is clear.

The clarification is due entirely to the evolution of the military establishment—in this country and others— since the end of World War II. The first thing to note about the two tomb figures is that they are soldiers, similarly dressed in classical armor, the "Active" one holding a marshal's baton, the "Contemplative" one with face shadowed by a helmet. The Active one holds a few coins in his hand; the Contemplative rests his elbow on a coin box. What Michelangelo is saying is that the military life has two, interchangeable sides, Active and Contemplative, and the Contemplative makes more money, requiring a box to hold it. Once we grasp this interpretation, it is almost superfluous to note that these two calm figures ("rather indolent": Wölfflin) preside over the four tortured forms beneath them, which, as Morning, Evening, Day and Night, represent the totality of human life lived in pain, sorrow and troubled sleep while in thrall to the military.

Michelangelo was speaking primarily of the Pentagon and its Russian complement, but, like all prophecies, his was founded on the experience of his own lifetime. In Renaissance Italy and even earlier, the beginnings had been made of the Contemplative Military Life which was to reach such Mannerist, Baroque and even Rococo expressions in our own time. Not counting such outsiders as the kings of France and Spain and the German emperor, the principal military class in Italy then was that of the *condottieri,* the professional soldiers for hire.

The Central and North Italians of the time were busy with many things. They had successfully brought into existence the city-state republics at total variance with the social structure of the rest of Europe. This new form had constantly to be attended. They had also, in the recent past, reinvented commerce and finance as channels of social movement and these both required vast amounts of attention. Besides all that, they had embarked on the most daring enterprise of all: they were creating the Renaissance. They had their hands full. At the same time they recognized that wars had to be carried on. There always had been wars. There always would be wars. Each generation of rulers accepted a measure of responsibility for continuing the tradition. So, busy with many things, they devised a typical Italian accommodation, as ingenious and useful as the fork and diplomacy, which they devised at about the same time. They devised the condottieri to fight their wars for them.

The condottieri are interesting and instructive for lots of reasons. For one thing they had more all-around class than any soldiers between Caesar and Napoleon. For another, they showed an early and constant tendency to try to take over the republics they were working for. They were also largely responsible for the revival of equestrian sculpture in bronze, providing in their persons the subjects, the models and the occasions. But the great thing about them, their supreme contribution to military thought, was their apparent realization that the Contemplative Life could be just as rewarding in the profession of arms as it could be anywhere. This was new. Until then everyone took it for granted that the soldier exemplified the Active Life, while the Contemplative Life was properly seen in the scholar, the hermit-monk, or even the poet. The condottieri stumbled into this profound insight and never had the chance fully to work it out, but it developed, however tentatively, as last year's ally became this year's foe, with the condottieri growing increasingly familiar with one another's styles in strategy. They fought wars of ground strategy with a lot of outflanking and countermarching, based, like the poetry and playwrighting of the period, on classical models. On more than one occasion individual captains, like an intelligent chess player, recognized that they had been outmaneuvered completely. Being, by the standards of the rest of Europe (and by our own) incredibly humane, they might then very well resign the game, or surrender, losing the war rather than several thousand additional lives.

The next step in the evolution would have been to plot out strategy on paper ahead of time, submit opposing plans to an impartial arbiter, appointed, perhaps, by the pope, or, more likely, by the sultan, and agree to accept his judgment as to which of the two battle plans would win. The step was never taken, although it was reached for. The French, Spanish and German barbarians all came roiling into the peninsula with the strategic finesse of Curtis Lemay: Nuke 'em! was the cry, but since the nukes hadn't been invented, the northerners made do with cannons and pikes and lots of bodies.

For a moment in the eighteenth century, the condottieri's discovery seemed about to emerge again, but the moment passed in the two revolutions which ended the century, the American and the French. The Americans refused to play war games with the British but shot from behind trees and stone walls like the plodding yeomen they were. The French destroyed the whole possibility of condottieri warfare by inventing universal conscription and that was that.

No one would have been more surprised than the original condottieri—and Michelangelo, for that matter —to find their—and his—astonishing conception finally realized when and where and by whom it has been, in post-World War II America by the military philosophers of the Pentagon. From the point of view of those Renaissance men, everything about the current situation is wrong as a setting for the condottieri idea. Their point of view is, in fact, quite correct and the original idea has been changed profoundly in its present-day embodiment. It has been so changed that it has become a burden instead of a boon for laboring mankind. Instead of transforming wars into essentially intellectual activities, it has made them more hopelessly material-oriented than ever. And it has, in a curious way, revived the ancient condottieri tendency to take over the republic employing them. But with all these subversions and inversions of the Rennaissance idea, the new style at the Pentagon is characterized by the technique of Research and Development, or R & D, and by the institution of the think tank, the outside group of brains to which problems are contracted out and even subcontracted out. The new style is therefore an authentic example of the Contemplative

Life expressed in the profession of arms. Michelangelo would not have been happy with the new military mutant; he certainly would not carve a statue of Herman Kahn, one of the first and still the best-known of the think tankers; but the sculptor would, however reluctantly, acknowledge that they all are the descendants of his shadowed figure, hand on chin, elbow on the box of coins, that sits in the basement of the Medici tombs.

What the paper condottieri of the Pentagon and the military philosophers of the think tanks do for a living is to dream up new combinations of weapons which the enemy—Russia or China, it hardly matters which—might very possibly think up some time in the next decade or two, and then dream up the logical strategic or tactical answer. The answers are invariably enormously costly even to start with. By the time they are finished, even in prototype, they cost two or three times the original vast estimates. The world of the Contemplative Military Man is, by definition, a world of hypothesis. The process of contemplation begins with a question: What if the Russians or the Chinese, ten years from now, come up with the incredible new weapon of knocking off edges of the moon and so timing the knockoffs that the eastern half of the United States can be thickly covered with moondust? Up to our eyeballs in moondust, we would be unable to grope our way to the underground controls of the Defense establishment and the Russians, or the Chinese, would have but to drop down out of the skies wearing their protective moondust masks and seize the bastion and citadel of the free world.

This is, certainly, an interesting intellectual exercise.

How do you stop them from chipping at the moon and dusting us with the chips? Granted that we must always avoid nuclear war, the obvious approach seems to be to mount a defensive system upon the moon's surface and to back it up with an earth-orbiting satellite system, both programmed to destroy any nuclear chippers that approach for a lunar landing. Together, these components constitute Phase I. In Phase II, the military philosophers must assume that the Russian or Chinese nuclear chippers—Commchips, they may be called for convenience —have eluded our double protective system and made it to the moon. In Phase II, therefore, the Americans concentrate on holding the moon together in one piece. This is most easily done by blasting our way into the moon's surface and injecting powerful, radioactive glue through its fissures and veins. Nevertheless, in spite of all this, there remains the fearful possibility that somehow, through their aggressive measures or our own defensive ones, a hunk of the moon will fall off, get pulverized into a cloud of dust and start drifting down to the Pentagon-West Point-Cambridge axis. This calls for Phase III and the creation, somehow, of a vast moondust umbrella, probably fashioned by exploding hydrogen bombs up in the stratosphere someplace where their force rays will spread out like the streamers from a skyrocket and neutralize the deadly dust.

Elaborating a scheme like that can take a summer afternoon or so of life among the paper condottieri in the think tanks. Working out the plans, making sure to get the flush valves in the right places and the input-output functioning efficiently, could go on for a year or more.

Then, actually going into production and making the moondust umbrellas and the other components can keep the appropriate businesses in business for a decade or more, and even call new ones into existence to take up any slack occasioned by the retirement of procurement officers at the Pentagon. But between the idea and the reality falls the shadow of Congress and the President. There was a time, as the historical-minded may recall, when the Indochina war was really a battle for men's minds. We are not fighting for land, the Army flacks used to hand out regularly, still less to destroy the enemy: we are fighting the battle for men's hearts and minds and we are winning. The flacks came by the phrase honestly enough, for their masters, the paper condottieri, are constantly engaged in the battle for men's minds. It's just on a somewhat smaller scale and an infinitely more important one than the battle fought by the poor propagandists attempting to tell the Vietnamese that having their villages blown up was good for them. The condottieri battle for the minds and the hearts of a few influential members of Congress, and of the President of the United States and his closest advisors, including, usually, his Secretary of Defense but not necessarily his Secretary of State.

How the heart and mind of an appropriate member of Congress are won may be studied in the late career of L. Mendel Rivers, from the substantial military projects that always ended up in Charleston, South Carolina, to the grand luxe living the military managed to produce along his fabled tours of inspection of home and foreign bases. It is an ancient story and not without its amusing

side if you don't mind having W. C. Fields in charge of
your life and fortune as well as your mind and heart.

The President and his crowd are more difficult, being,
on average, more intelligent and a lot more alert to possible political peril than are Congressmen who have
adorned the Capitol for decades. So far, however, they
have never failed to respond, like Pavlov's dogs, to the
brazen alarm bell telling of impending defeat, disaster
and destruction. "I shall not be the first President of the
United States to lose a war," is one of those standing
declarations that ought to be printable from a single key
on the ghostly typewriters of Presidential speechmen.

That awful threat of establishing the Presidential precedent for defeat is supposedly what has kept us in Indochina so long and so expensively. But that is in the
Active Life and the Active Life, in the new military
world of the Pentagon, is not nearly as important as the
Contemplative. In the Contemplative Life, that magic
formula about losing wars is totally open-ended, hence
the coin box under the thinking soldier's elbow. When a
beleaguered general from the field employs the formula,
he is talking about more bombing or an old-fashioned
battleship to sail up and down the coast in the hope of
invoking victory by the veneration of cult objects formerly efficacious. When the Pentagon's paper condottieri say the words, they mean big money, minimum accounting for it, built-in escalation of costs, and no
guarantee whatever that the magic system being contracted for will accomplish its magic. In fact, there is
just about, by now, a guarantee that it will not. In the
first place, it may not work at all, in the most basic,

elementary sense in which your automobile doesn't work —or your washing machine or whatever other machines you have to make the living more easy. Assuming it does, which is quite an assumption, it is almost certain that no machine, no weapons system, no military magic, is going, finally and forever, to give absolute protection to the United States against whatever horrors the Russians or Chinese may dream up, or, to phrase it more accurately, against whatever horrors the paper condottieri may dream that the Russians or Chinese may dream. Their world of hypothesis mysteriously loses its if-ness between the think tank and the congressional hearing room. Molière somewhere has a routine between a con man and a bumpkin in which the sharper works the line: if a thing can happen, it must have potential for happening, but potential is the essence of reality, for without potential nothing could actually be; therefore, if something could happen, it virtually has happened and we must proceed on the basis that, in fact, it really has happened. The routine is played regularly in military limousines on the short rides from the Pentagon to Capitol Hill and the White House. What began as an interesting intellectual supposition to while away a summer's day at a think tank up the Hudson or in sunny California becomes, by the time the Congress or the President hear of it, an absolute certainty. The Russians are coming, the Russians are coming, with their magical moondust machine! You wouldn't want to be the first President to lose a war. Up the nuclear umbrellas.

There is, of course, a checking mechanism for all this. It is called the Intelligence Community and it is not a smart town, but simply the top people in the CIA and the other spook outfits in Washington, mostly service-connected. We still tend to think of spooks as climbing fire escapes to steal papers and some of that goes on, sure enough. But most of the work in the spook shops consists of analyzing information that is more or less available to anyone who takes the trouble to find it. The trick is not so much getting up the fire escape and into the hidden drawer in the desk as in finding the right pieces in a jigsaw puzzle that extends to infinity, in getting any six or eight of them to fit together long enough to mean something to someone someplace in the Intelligence Community. Granted that, the subornation of any part of the community is almost automatic. American industry, too, has its intelligence community and while some members of it no doubt do climb fire escapes and steal sketches of next year's designs, most of them are engaged in far more pedestrian tasks. They are engaged in assembling the data that will prove the course the advertising agency is urging its client to embark upon is absolutely right and the only possible way to deal with the threat or opportunity or doldrums now presenting itself to the industry as a whole. Somewhere, no doubt—perhaps in such questions as the frequency of the aorist tense in the orations of Demosthenes—research is carried on in order to find something out. In military-political affairs, it has long been a tool of persuasion rather than an instrument of investigation. The point of military research, like that of advertising research, is to support what has already been determined, namely, the need to increase the budget. No motivation researcher working for Madison Avenue ever brought in a conclusion that no further advertising was needed, the product was well enough known already. Similarly, no military affairs researcher employed by the Intelligence Community of the United States ever concluded that the proposed new weapons system was not, after all, a vital and absolute and immediate necessity.

So much for the checking mechanism. It's like asking a motorcar salesman for his honest, off-the-record opinion of his product. It is not that he would conceal such an opinion, but simply that such a thing does not exist. His opinion is formed after his conclusion is accepted and is shaped precisely to support that conclusion. There is no Consumer Reports Service in the military-political-industrial complex and one is desperately needed. The Intelligence Community, for example, at the beginning of the decade of the sixties, was quite certain the Bay of Pigs invasion would be a smashing success instead of just a smash. At the end of that decade the same community was assuring the country that the Russians were building a submarine base in Cuba which would have to be countered. What both "certainties" had in common was the need to spend a lot of money through military channels.

There is an essential difference between those Renaissance Italian condottieri in their silky-satiny scarlet and gold and the think tankers in their drab sack suits. Right from the start the Italians were in business to save their employers money, time and effort. They would, like most people, grab anything that was there for the grabbing, like the independence of the republic. But if that thought did not occur to them, or if they rejected it as improbable of success or simply too complicated, then there was no question of their position and function in relation to the state. They existed for the sake of the state. They existed so that the state might be free to go about its other concerns: the import-export business between Samarkand and Switzerland, the lending, servicing and collection of moneys to assorted princely dignitaries bent on enhancing their princeliness or their dignity, and, of course, creating the Renaissance. The condottiere took his pay and did his work and once in a way got his effigy modeled in clay and cast in bronze upon a bronze horse set on a pedestal in front of a church. But always, he knew his place, as they used to say down South in Dixie. If he seized his chance and seized the state, then, like Louis later, he *was* the state and acted thereafter from stately motives, no longer from merely military ones. Not so with our own paper condottieri. It has all been turned upside down. The purposes of the state have been subsumed in the purposes of the military establishment, though the two are by no means as identical as is commonly assumed, and may often be antithetical.

The assumed identity of purpose is easy enough to understand. It has a curious parallel in the assumption, also military in origin, that the best needs and desires of our sons in service are best served by our support of their masters. One of the most enduring arguments for our presence in Vietnam has been the support of American boys: we have to keep our troops in Vietnam to protect our troops in Vietnam. The argument has an engaging quality about it, rather like one of the circular arguments

Vice President Agnew makes against liberal Republicans who are just as bad as liberal Democrats who are just as bad as liberal Republicans. When we move from ingenious argument to factual reporting, we find, not unexpectedly, that the serviceman who has fought and bled for his country is regularly shortchanged by the military establishment and by the government which claims to be carrying on the war in his name. Veterans' hospitals are pitifully inadequate; veterans' benefits are fragmentary and ineffective compared to the benefits that daily accrue to any retired procurement officer with the wit or the memory to join a firm selling to the Pentagon or to found his own. It is the same in the broader assumption of identity of purpose between the American state, let alone the American society, and the American military establishment. In pure logic, the two things ought to be the same in effort. The military, surely, exists for the sake of the larger community which maintains it. Yet, in practice, things get turned around. The military exists to save the state and the society, but the threat is so grave that both state and society must be destroyed to some extent—the whole bill isn't in yet and won't be for generations—in order to be saved by the military. There remains the philosophical question of what it is that is saved when that which was to be saved is destroyed by the process of saving it.

The classical condottiere, when taking over the state which he had signed on to serve, would usually do so as the result of a grand victory over the state's foes. Sweeping the field before him, he would return to the metropolis and either accept the engineered demands of the people that he assume their leadership in peace since he had managed it so brilliantly in war, or, more bluntly, remind the elders that he was the commander of all the force there was and wished to be named Lord Protector and Duke. Subtle or straightforward, his change in status from instrument to primary person was based on victory in the field. So has it been in America with those generals who have acceded to the office of chief magistrate of the republic. From Washington to Eisenhower, without exception, they have gained the confidence of their countrymen from the quality of their performance in the field. And, despite the prophets of gloom and doom on the left, the republic has survived every inauguration of every victorious general who has come home to lead the nation in peace as he had in war.

In theory these military men were supposed to suborn the republic into something different, sterner, less free. In practice none of them did so. Washington, landed gent and would-be capitalist, had other things to think about. Jackson, although a general, was the most democratic of leaders. Harrison, poor chap; Grant, amiable drunkard. Eisenhower, of all people, was the one President in the history of the republic to warn the people against the military-industrial complex. Everyone else in the years before and since, including and especially the passionate liberals, Kennedy and Johnson, couldn't debase themselves fast enough or completely enough before the overwhelming ends of military purpose.

We have not become a military state by subversion on the part of military Presidents. We have certainly not become a military state in popular response to military vic-

tories. We have, instead, become a military state out of
the sheer incompetence of the military. They come before us, or before our elected representatives, and con-
fess, more or less annually, that the problems they are
paid to handle are beyond their handling and therefore
they need more of everything: more men, more rank,
more science, more research, more think tankers, more
paper condottieri, and, always and everywhere, more
money. Like some hopeless, drunken uncle, they seduce
us by their inability to make anything work and come
around every year to pick up the handout and blackmail
us into raising the ante. The American soul has always
been a soft touch for a hard luck story, but surely this is
the first time in our history or in anyone else's when the
panhandler, down on his luck, was invited in to run the
show.

This, perhaps, is the supreme advantage of the Contemplative Life as a branch of the profession of arms. In
the olden times a soldier had to win big to get much of
anything in the way of subverting the state or even a pension appreciably above the union scale. Nowadays, the
worse they are, the better they are. Or at least, the better
off they are. The Soldier as Contemplative, by taking
thought, has accrued to himself power and pelf never
dreamt of by his predecessors in the Active Life. He has
but to think, and then to counterthink, to unleash the
golden rain of the United States Treasury upon him and
his schemes.

In the purest theory of the paper condottieri, the
American war in Vietnam and the incursion in Cambodia
and the outing in Laos and so on, all these were doubt-

less mistakes. In theory, the military mind addresses itself to the supreme abstract problems of the age, What shall we do if the Russians start chipping away the moon? and questions of that ilk. These are the considerations—fundamentally unanswerable—that sprinkle stars on the shoulders and expand the ever-expanding table of organization. But, as Michelangelo showed in that tomb, the Contemplative Life is insupportable without the Active Life marching alongside, step by step. Vietnam, at the bearable cost of a great deal of national tumult, has given the military establishment the abiding, daily proof that their sketches of science-fiction futures—which would otherwise strike anyone as demented ravings—have the leverageable, negotiable advantage of possible truth.

Except for Michelangelo, the last people to combine the Active Life and the Contemplative Life as a matter of high policy were the Benedictine monks in the sixth century and after. They used the combination to modulate Europe from the Dark Ages to the High Middle Ages by draining fens and teaching literacy for the love of God. The monks, in their combination, began with barbarism and climbed up to civilization. The paper condottieri in the Pentagon are beginning with civilization and God help us all.

The Godless Atheists

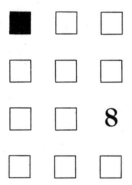

"The specter of Communism is stalking Europe," said Karl Marx, the old gypsy man, shaking his gory locks and rattling his chains. A hundred years later the ghost has gone west. The specter of Communism is stalking the Pentagon and never was a shade more welcome. Marx and his disciples walk those miles of halls each night like Anne Boleyn in the Tower of London. Like impoverished peers in England, the Pentagon proprietors take in a little more because the stately home is haunted. In fact, they take in a lot more. Truth to tell, if it weren't for Communism, the place would have been out of business long ago, the great warren of a building turned over to urban rehabilitation or human rehabilitation or any of the monumental tasks we keep putting off because of the ghosts in the corridors.

Karl Marx, of course, didn't know anymore about Communism as it has come into existence than Jesus Christ knew about Vatican protocol, or Henry Ford about air pollution. Marx had a burning faith that the nineteenth-century industrial capitalism he studied with such loathing in Germany and England was bound to collapse of its own inner contradictions and lead to the establishment of Communism as a kind of receivership state. Nothing remotely like that happened at all. Instead, the sleeping giant of Europe, backward old Russia, collapsed into a homemade revolution which, thanks chiefly to the machinations of the Imperial German High Command, got stolen by Lenin and his Bolsheviks. Far from inheriting the corrupt riches of industrial capitalism, Communism as it came into being inherited the corrupt poverty of the last great feudal society. The Bolsheviks were victims of the time warp, coming to power approximately four centuries ahead of where they should have in the Marxist scheme of social evolution. For this and for other reasons, including personal taste, Lenin revived Terror as an instrument of government, Trotsky created the Red Army as a missionary society, and Stalin invented the ideological novelty of Communism in One Country. Each of these personal contributions has had a great deal more to do with shaping Communism than anything Marx ever wrote. But the most important shaping factor of all has been the time warp: In Marx's proprietary pride, natural enough, Communism is the inevitable successor to capitalism and that, of course, is what gives Americans and other sensitive capitalist states the heebie-jeebies; that's what walks the Pentagon at night and floods it with fructifying money during the day. In fact, the relationship is exactly the other way around. Communism is not the successor to capitalism, it is the predecessor to capitalism or, at most, a kind of alternative procedure for bringing societies along from relatively primitive social-economic organization to relatively sophisticated social-economic organization.

In truth, if any Western capitalist ideologue were fractionally as dedicated to the grand old cause of capitalism as the freebee ads of the Advertising Council and the editorials in the *Reader's Digest* suggest everybody is, he could hardly find a modern phenomenon more fascinating and flattering to study than Communism. When there was still a functioning Communist Party of America, the weary hacks in charge of it in the mid-Stalinist period of purges used to assert tirelessly that "Communism is twentieth-century democracy." They were even capable of developing the thought for a thousand words or so at the drop of a question, but the statement, of course, was pure Orwellian of a fairly high order, a bland assertion that opposite things are really the same thing. They could, however, have made a very strong case for a related proposition: Communism is twentieth-century capitalism. Whatever Marx may have had in mind, Communism in practice has been essentially an elaborate, often cumbersome and inefficient, but totally dedicated apparatus for the accumulation of capital.

Capital, in the use shared by Adam Smith and Karl Marx, is the labor surplus that may be used for other things than the sustenance of the labor that produced it, especially for the financing of still further production. The dream of capitalism is basically the dream of the milkmaid on her way to the market: with the proceeds of the milk, I'll buy a hen; with the proceeds from the eggs, I'll get a churn; with the butter money, I'll buy a bull and so on. The ending of the story, the spilling of the milk, turns it all into a human drama and a bit of homely wisdom, but up to then, the story is the theory of capitalism. At a certain point in such accumulations, what we have since learned to call a critical mass appears, which abruptly becomes self-generating, in the style of a nuclear explosion. The critical mass of capitalism appeared in Western Europe toward the end of the eighteenth century, with the perfection of things like the spinning jenny, Cartwright's loom and Watt's steam engine. Here were sources of so much labor surplus that the whole economic structure changed violently. A second critical mass appeared in America in the decades following the Civil War, and a third in the electronics-nuclear-computer decades after the Second World War. The entire effort of the Soviet Union, during its first half century of existence, has been to bring about the accumulation of a first critical mass, while at the same time dealing with the technical developments of the second and third from the West. Obviously, anyone who really puts any stock in the theory of capitalism as a living faith could not but be sympathetically fascinated at the Soviet effort to get capitalized a couple of hundred years late.

The paucity of such interest on the part of dedicated capitalists in America suggests that they really are not all that dedicated to capitalism. Their dedication is to something else, either self-interest in the narrowest of senses or in some broader sense. At any rate, it ought to be clear that, at bottom, far from there being any intrinsic conflict between capitalism and Communism, the two systems are the same thing, at different times. The savagery of Lenin's Terror against his own citizens, raised to paranoiac levels by Stalin and still an uneasy part of the Soviet system, compares not too unfavorably with the treatment of working men, women and children as portrayed in the novels of Charles Dickens or the photos of Lewis Hine. If capitalism is the accumulation of labor surplus, one obvious way to increase the surplus has always been to take it out of the sustenance of the labor. At that top, ideological level it is obvious that war, or the threat of war, between capitalism and Communism, can only get credibility from more or less deliberate efforts to obscure the basic identity of the two different brand names for the rapid accumulation of working capital.

As it happened, both sides had plenty of reason to obscure that identity and to portray the other as a natural, implacable enemy. At the start of Communism in Russia, the Soviets found themselves invaded by foreign devils in support of the "Whites," the czarist forces, in the hope of keeping Russia in the war against Germany and Austria. Hence, it was easy and natural to portray all the West as "counterrevolutionary" and dedicated to the destruction of the Soviet Motherland. On our side, Bolshevism, as it was still called, was quite clearly a device by the German High Command to knock out one of our allies. Equally naturally, we looked askance at the new society that was struggling to be carpentered together in Petrograd and its provinces. It wasn't that America was all that pro-czarist, anymore than, later, we were all that pro-Batista. It was just that word of Marxian attacks on our kind of society had come filtering across the Atlantic, starting with Marx's own dispatches as European correspondent for the old New York *Herald*. It was the time warp again. The society Marx was attacking was almost unknown to Americans in the 1920s, yet he used the same names for it as they used for their own. The same confusion obtained on the other side: since Western Europe and America were clearly capitalist and imperialist, they were also the monsters described by Marx. And so it has gone, a curse upon international understanding, but the greatest possible blessing for paper condottieri on both sides of the Iron Curtain.

Even something as obviously a matter for a people's own concern as Soviet atheism has been brought into court against Communism in America. The fact is, of course, that Russian reaction against the state church is an exaggerated version of the American doctrine of the separation of Church and State. Both are equally heretical, novel and dangerous—from the point of view of most European societies until quite recently. In Europe it has always been assumed that the interests of Church and State are identical. The assumption, modified but intact, survives in such contemporary phenomena as the position of Elizabeth II, a horsewoman of some attainment, as the head of the Church of England, and the long struggle of Italians for freedom to obtain divorce. In America the relationship between the two institutions has deliberately been made quite different, the Church being a theoretically private institution with almost no official relations with the State. In Russia, the Church has been treated more harshly, but then the Church in Russia had been much more closely allied with the former management. Official atheism is, in the view of many American churchmen of not too many years ago, a difference of degree, not of kind, from official ecclesiastical neutrality on the part of the State, such as has always been American policy. They were right: from the European perspective that comprises the major share of the history of Christianity, official neutrality is barely distinguishable from official atheism. The effect of both is the same, to remove affairs of state from ecclesiastical concern. When we remember the Wars of Religion, the Thirty Years' War, the Holy Inquisition, the Star Chamber, the Salem Witch Trials, the Crusades, Prohibition and Dr. Carl McIntyre, we see that there is much to be said for official atheism, almost as much as there is to be said for Separation, the American Way.

Ah, Dr. McIntyre: an embarrassment at times but the invaluable support of the whole military structure of the United States in its present form as crypto-military-dictatorship. Dr. McIntyre, with his Marches for Victory and his easy identification of the United States with all that is good, the Soviet Union with all that is evil, is the most solid support the Pentagon has in its own tacit yet absolute assumption that the only way to deal with the Soviets is with nukes and the threat of nukes. Like the

Soviets, we have a time warp of our own and Dr. Mc-
Intyre is the very woof of our warp. Our time warp isn't as
bad as theirs, for while theirs stretches back to before
America was even a nation, ours only warps around to
1910 or so. Until that time, Americans lived in a world
complete unto itself. What was foreign was evil, almost
by definition and always by experience. There had been
the odd Washington Irving or Henry Adams hankering
after foreign gods, but such Americans *were* odd: the
main thrust was westward and inward, ourselves to ourselves. The two big wars of this century changed a lot of
that, bringing Europe and even parts of Latin America
into the American family. But the essential xenophobia
remains, directed now against Russia and China, the Red
Menace and the Yellow Peril, the better suited to the
purpose for their being officially atheists. In 1910 we
could simply turn our backs on the stuck-up English and
the papist Italians. In the 1970s Dr. McIntyre translates
the same basic attitude into foreign intervention of every
sort and the Pentagon, for all its occasional embarrassment at his frankness, is well served.

Wars, however, are not really fought—or haven't been
until now—over ideological questions. They are fought
over reality, as in the expression *real property*. The
casual observer, confronting a map of the world or even
a globe, would be hard put to find an obvious point of
potential trouble between the Russians and the Americans. The Russians could naturally fight with the Chinese and with the whole file of countries in Eastern
Europe from Finland to Turkey. They have borders
with them all and have fought them all. We, on the other

hand, could reasonably go to war with the Mexicans, and have done so, or with the Canadians—but for some reason have not yet done so on any serious scale. Both Russia and America could go to war with the Germans, the Germans being what they are, and both have done so. But for Russia and America to fight each other for any kind of rational purpose, or even for the two great countries to be normally belligerent, would take a heap of doing, cartographically speaking.

There are no common boundaries, no territories irredenta—unless you count Alaska, which is by now pretty much a lost cause for the expansion of the Russian Empire. On the map, in terms of the classical causes of war, there would seem to be almost no way to get America and Russia involved in hostilities or even hostile feelings. That it has been managed is certainly one of the great achievements of war lovers on both sides. Despite the incredibility of it all, we find ourselves locked into a kind of permanent confrontation or near-confrontation with the Russians, and they with us. Both of us, moreover, are edging into the same situation as regards the Chinese. The time warp is mainly responsible, both the time warp backward, which involves both of us seeing the other in terms of realities that no longer exist, and the time warp forward, which involves enormous investments in weapons for the future, which must then be justified by the future, which is then manipulated to do so.

Both the world empires have dabbled in the local politics of what are laughingly called the new republics of Africa and Asia, or, just as comically, the older ones of Latin America. But most of the dabbling has been predicated on the need of each to outdabble the other. It has been responsive dabbling, rather than initiative dabbling. We, for example, got in up to our eyeballs in Vietnam presumably to keep the Russians and/or the Chinese out of there, while both the Russians and the Chinese stood gratefully aside and allowed us to flounder around, shooting up our ammunition, killing our own troops and laying waste the countryside. We never laid a glove on them because they weren't there to hit, but they might have been and we got in there to keep them out. We must, at any rate have gone in there for some reason and that one is as good as any that anyone can now remember. We anticipated.

On the other hand, we have never lifted a finger to prevent actual Russian takeovers of all the East European nations, even Czechoslovakia, the one authentic democracy in the lot during the interwar period. Similarly, when the Russians moved into Egypt and began kidding the Egyptians that they were good enough to take the Israelis in the seventeenth or eighteenth round, again, we moved very cautiously indeed. To be sure, in Korea we made the hideous mistake of giving Douglas MacArthur his head; he took the war up to the Yalu and immediately the Red Chinese came pouring across the Yalu with drums and bugles. But except for that, we have been extremely circumspect in our relations with the big Communist nations. There is a strange discrepancy between our announced policies of containing Communism and our actual encounters with the chief Communist nations. In practice, we go after the smaller ones: North Vietnam, the local organizations in South Vietnam, Laos and Cambodia, and, of course, through economic warfare, Cuba.

The two powers thus seem to have drifted, more or less consciously, into a pattern like that of two heavyweight boxers knocking the hell out of each other in different rings. We're shadow-boxing like Battling McGurk while issuing statements like Mohammad Ali, only not as well-phrased.

Obviously, this is preferable to the real thing, although it is rather a strain on the nerves. And it is a strain on a lot more than the nerves of the helpless taxpayer in America. It is a severe strain on the economies of both the superpowers and on the entire world, which desperately needs the surplus energy created by the superpower economies to feed people around the globe and eventually to lead them to the point at which they can feed themselves.

Even from our own official devil theory of Communism, the permanent channeling off of our treasure and youth into war and its simulacrum as elaborated by the paper condottieri is precisely the wrong thing to do. It is all very well for Communist prophets from Marx to Khrushchev to proclaim the inevitability of Communism, but it is not inevitable in the least. It is not at all a logical development of a capitalist society in its normal functioning. It is, almost without exception, a product of war and the social confusion wrought by a really catastrophic war. The confusion wrought by World War I, for example, was not enough, finally, to turn either Germany or Hungary Communist, although Communists in both places made a good try. But the same war brought confusion enough to Russia to allow Communism to triumph. There was no question of Russian Communism triumphing in Eastern Europe after World War II: that was Trotsky's Red Army, at last going international, as he had always said it should. But Yugoslavia, an authentic Communist nation—as opposed to the imported Communism of East Europe—could only have come into its Communist existence in the total chaos created by the invasion of the Balkans by Hitler. North Vietnam, another authentic Communist nation, likewise came into existence in the chaos created by the war against Japan and against the French, the two foreign invaders. China, too, the second big one, would never have become Communist without the military invasion by the anti-Communist Japanese. Clearly, Communism, besides being twentieth-century capitalism, is also twentieth-century nationalism. This is a truth that the Russians must know by now, although they are slow to admit it. It is a truth that the United States has to come to terms with eventually. When we do, we shall begin the dismantlement of the Pentagon. It may well be that that logical, inevitable corollary of the simple, obvious truth that Communism is not an international unified movement directed primarily against the United States is what keeps us from accepting it.

But the evidence is overwhelming. Like Christianity, Communism is a very fragmentary thing. Amish people believe—the more devout, at least—that purity of conscience is somehow connected with black buggies drawn by horses over dirt roads; the Cardinal Archbishop of New York takes a limousine for granted. Dr. Billy Graham, the nearest thing to a gray eminence we have, believes that Jesus Christ will very likely return to earth any minute now and inaugurate a reign of peace and justice; Rev. Carl McIntyre, equally fundamentalist, believes that we must smite the Commies hip and thigh and not wait for Jesus to do it. Tennessee preachers handle snakes and testify thus to the power of the Lord; Orthodox theologians handle subtle structures of reason assembled by John Chrysostom and Basil the Great. All these people call themselves Christians and you are welcome to try to sign them all up for cooperative endeavor in *any* enterprise. Many Protestants regard gambling as the gaud of Satan; many Catholics absolutely depend upon Bingo to keep the Roman establishment going. Most Protestants think of birth control as a normal, natural, essential part of modern marriage; most Catholic officials denounce it as diabolical in origin, worse than Bingo. Sure, they're all Christians, but good luck, pal, in getting them together in anything more complicated then replenishing the local hospital's blood bank. And even there . . .

So it is with Communism. The time warp, as always, sets the scene. When the Russians invaded Czechoslovakia in 1968, they issued a statement of justification that might have been composed by any of the sixteenth-century popes seeking to maintain Christian unity. The Dubcek government had gone too far too fast in the wrong direction. The Russians, as the original copyright holders, had the final word on what was Communism and what was not. With brotherly concern, they were coming to the aid of loyal Czechs by invading the country. The Czechs were peculiarly suited to be the recipients of the Russian crocodile tears at the necessity of invasion, for they had received exactly the same sort of sympathy from the Catholic-imperialist forces invading Bohemia in the seventeenth century to save Czechs from Czech Christianity, or Protestantism.

The sixteenth-century Christian problem and the twentieth-century Communist problem are much the same. Communism, it would seem, is not only twentieth-century capitalism and twentieth-century nationalism, it is also twentieth-century Christianity in its hope of heaven, its would-be universality, and its fragmentation at the hands of as many national interpreters—or heretics, or deviationists—as there are nations.

Taken all in all, Yugoslavia is probably the best-situated Communist state there is, from the point of view of some occult balance to be struck between general economic welfare and specific human freedom, the two basic values that are so often in conflict in any system. Yugoslavia got where it is under the determined leadership of a man highly trained in Moscow to be a creature of the international Communist conspiracy, as we would call it, to bring the South Slavs into the great gathering of Soviet Slavic peoples with headquarters in Moscow. Tito at home labored away and would have got absolutely nowhere except for the Nazi invasion. He emerged as the only national leader willing and able to fight the Germans, and hence ended up as the leader of the liberated country. He immediately began detaching himself from Moscow. The Red Army, Trotsky's evangelical instrument, never took over in Yugoslavia because Tito's Communists stood ready to fight the Russians as they had fought the Germans. Clearly, something was operating within Tito and his colleagues other than devotion to international Communist solidarity. The fact is, evidenced in the sad history of East Europeans throwing rocks at Russian tanks, that all Communist societies tend toward the independence achieved by Tito's. The difference is that Tito fought for and won his country; the others had theirs handed to them by the Red Army and it just isn't the same.

With all the improbabilities of Russia and America squaring off at each other and drifting into a permanent state of hostility, one cause is somewhere close to the root of it all. That is the rivalry for position as successor to Rome as prime organizer of the world. The Russians take a strong line as the direct descendant of Byzantium, which was the direct descendant of Rome. We disparage their lineage. The Turks, who conquered Byzantium, have a better claim to that particular line than the Russians do and who hears a peep out of the Turks? Our own claims rest upon a felt affinity more than anything else. Look at the architecture of Washington, D.C., for heaven's sake. If the Russians are the Third Rome, how come St. Basil's looks like something in an amusement park? Washington, in contrast, from the Supreme Court to the Capitol to the Archives and National Gallery, could all have come out of any nineteenth-century American survey of Roman culture. In the twentieth century the American air voyager looks down upon a nationwide pattern of concrete ribbons of superhighways and blue rectangles of swimming pools and recalls that the Romans, too, were noted for their roads and for their baths.

The rivalry is deceptive. There isn't going to be a Third

Rome, or, if there is, it certainly isn't going to be either Russia or America as now constituted. We Americans pulled Europe up from the ashes of World War II and cannot really count on any European country to be with us in, say, Vietnam. The Russians, they like to think, created Castro's Cuba, but even there they cannot rely on the Maximum Leader to follow the Russian pattern.

Stalin, villain that he may have been, had the wit to perceive, as Trotsky did not, that Communism in One Country was the only possible way for Soviet Russia to come into viable existence. His formula has been enthusiastically accepted by every Communist nation or regime since then. Even Communist Albania, never especially noted for its astuteness in world or Balkan affairs, had the wit very early on to declare itself Communist on the Chinese model, thus at once fending off Russia and Yugoslavia. When the Egyptians in their madness began their strange alliance with Russia, the terrorist Arab army, the fedayeen, immediately opened relations with Red China. China itself, of course, despite decades of material and instructional—"advisory," as we used to say in Vietnam—help from Russia, had hardly ousted Chiang from the mainland before it declared its Communist independence of Russia. The awful truth is that there isn't any Communist international. It's a ghost to frighten Congressmen.

Diocletian, as noted above, when he wasn't throwing Christians to the lions in the hope of getting an afternoon's sport, was splitting the Roman Empire into the division that still endures, with opposing capitals now undreamed of then, Moscow and Washington. His successor, Constantine the Great, took a step equally imaginative in coping with the problems of his time. Since it wasn't working, he abandoned Diocletian's traditionalist, conservative, pious policy of killing Christians. Instead, he allied the state with the new religion and thus gained a life of better than a thousand years for a society that, when he took the step, was tottering on the edge of oblivion.

Clearly, alliance between American and Russia is still too outrageous from either side's pious, conservative, traditionalist point of view. But it remains the only final alternative to the military games we play while the world sinks slowly into doom.

First Aid and Last Rites

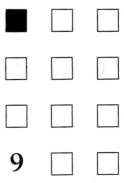

9

When Andrew Carnegie, the old rascal, felt like giving
a million dollars to some nutty scheme for saving Scot-
land from the English, he handed over the money and
that was that. Carnegie's motives in getting rid of the
substantial amount of money he did get rid of were mildly
complex, running from his famous "Gospel of Wealth,"
according to which a man was supposed to be ashamed
to die rich, to a genuine personal interest in the particular
philanthropy, such as the hero awards, the libraries and
the bonnie braes. However, when John D. Rockefeller
the First, at least as great a rascal as Carnegie, felt like

handing out a dime or two to passersby on his birthday, he had to have a public relations man—the first public relations man, in fact, Ivy Lee—tell him it was an okay thing because it would improve the image. Sure enough, a bare three generations later, Rockefellers are pop political heroes in New York, West Virginia and Arkansas, not bad image-repairing for an old duck whom many of his contemporaries would gladly have lynched as an early step in a national beautification program.

Still, successful as it was, Old Rocky's free and easy way with the dime has cast its shadow over all of American politics of the post-World War II era, with special reference to the Russian-American standoff and the consequent development of the Big Soldier as a major item in the American annual budget.

There is another antecedent in the same line, the American missionary. The American missionary society, as it evolved in the nineteenth century, was not just the pious enterprise we read about in Louisa May Alcott and James Michener. It was, in the history of missionary work, a revolutionary departure from precedent. Consider some of the precedents: Peter and Paul, of course, rank high in any honor roll of missionaries, splitting out from Jerusalem to all over the Middle East, and finally, inevitably, to Rome, the center of civilization, to preach the word of God. They brought nothing with them but that word and their trades of fisherman and tentmaker; they lived off the land and hoped for the best. By contrast, the Catholic missionaries to South America, and the Anglican ones to India a bit later, came marvelously equipped with everything contemporary technology had to offer, but they weren't offering it to their new flock. The flock, in fact, was there for shearing and the missionary endeavors of both the Spanish and the English nations were intimately involved with the shearers. Christianity, from the strict cost-accounting point of view of the people with the shears in Peru or Burma, was useful because it preached resignation to one's lot and it taught the language of the shearer. There were thus established the two basic modes of the missionary endeavor: the propertyless preacher coming to a strange land, often one of a much higher culture than his own, offering only the word of God as he has heard it, and the missionary as part of the general apparatus of conquest, with the word of God rather thoroughly mixed up with the word of the East India Company of Merchant-Adventurers or their most Catholic Majesties of Spain. The nineteenth-century American missionary society was something else—among other things, it was a form of bribery.

The missionary endeavor sent forth from and financed by the nineteenth-century American Christian community was the first on any substantial scale to offer something to its prospective converts besides the word of God and membership in the ecclesiastical society of the missionary. Food, clothing and medical supplies poured forth from sewing circles and church picnics in New England and the Midwest to the naked natives of the Congo and the broad Pacific. At every level, from the meeting of the sewing circle back in Concord, Massachusetts, to the dispensation of goods in the jungle, there was a well-understood trading relationship. So many bales of goods, so many "souls," a new variation on Chichikov's purchases of "dead souls" in rural Russia. These were live ones. These were, you might say, the minds and hearts of the people. It was a precedent to which America would return.

The return took place in those formative years following World War II, when so much that has governed our lives since was decided upon or drifted into. We had come out of the war with a large and expressive minority of liberal, mostly Democratic, political activists caught up in the vision of the entire world as subject to the processes of plenty that had brought America so swiftly up from the Great Depression into its wartime status as the Arsenal of Democracy. Future wars, it was said, could almost be predicted in terms of population pressures and hunger quotients. It should easily be possible to head off universal starvation with the agricultural, commercial, financial know-how that America had to such a high degree. Why should people in distant lands starve in an age of prosperity? It seems somewhat strange, now, to recall that concern for foreign starvation, expressed in the apparent assumption of domestic plenty for all, but in those days the domestic problem of poverty was thought to have been pretty well solved by the New Deal and the prosperity engendered by World War II.

A little later another group of Americans began to become extremely alarmed over what they regarded as the Communist threat to the United States. These observers, who eventually included Senator Joseph R. McCarthy as their most famous member, pointed to Soviet expansion in East Europe, to active and ambitious Communist parties all over the world, and to the emergence of the Communists, after all our support to the brave

Generalissimo, as the absolute rulers of China. These observers also noted that here in the United States there were dangerously Communist-like persons and programs in and out of the government. These anti-Communists shortly began a program of hanging the blame for Communist expansionism on a handful of Washington bureaucrats and expert consultants. In the case of the consultants, they were for the most part accused of having reported to State and other departments that the Chinese Communists were unquestionably the strongest force in postwar mainland China. When this proved indeed to be the case, these consultants were felt, by virtue of their accurate advice, to have actually brought that situation into existence. They were accused of having "sold out" Chiang and China to Mao and the other Chinese. The anti-Communists in America at that time believed, on the one hand, that the international Communist conspiracy was omniscient and omnipotent in its uncanny apparatus of knowing and doing around the world and, on the other hand, that that same international conspiracy couldn't know or do a thing without the treasonous cooperation of Americans of liberal persuasion. The two propositions, of course, contradicted each other absolutely, but this did not stop the anti-Communists from proceeding on the two fronts without relating either to the other. Domestic traitors or possible traitors were hunted down as if all depended upon finding them; and at the same time, the beginnings of the arms race were pushed vigorously under such prestige as that of Edward Teller. The two programs, contradictory in assumptions, came together in the denial of security clearance to Dr. Oppenheimer lest he discover what he had already discovered. It was a heady season.

Suddenly the sweet, perhaps somewhat naive, dream of international liberals, satirized as "a quart of milk on every Arab's doorstep," seemed in quite possibly fatal danger from the revived and virulent anti-Communism that fell upon Alger Hiss and Mao alike, without much discrimination between the two. The dream of a just world seemed quite likely to vanish in the smoke of weapons tests and weapons employment as well. The whole grisly structure of the power establishment before World War II seemed on the point of resurrection, with different players, to be sure, but the same in essence, piling up arms until it seemed absurd not to be using them. At this point, moved by what seemed to everyone the purest kind of inspiration, liberal voices took up a new refrain, a chorus that managed, miraculously, to subsume the new anti-Communism into the old humanitarianism of the original aid proposals.

The new line for proponents of foreign aid was that it was the most effective kind of anti-Communism. As a matter of fact, foreign aid is not particularly effective as a preventive or remedy to Communism; further, the ingenious adaptation of the generous impulse to the paranoid obsession cast a shadow over foreign aid that has been there ever since, and has effectively prevented it from achieving any of the goals that might have reasonably been expected.

As to the first point, the theory of aid as anti-Communism assumes that impoverished nations are uniformly composed of citizens sitting around ready to "go

Communist" in desperation if nothing better turns up. By pouring aid into such nations, the theory runs, the citizens can have their minds deflected into healthier channels and begin to build prosperity for themselves. The truth, insofar as we know it, is considerably more complex. The relationship between hunger-despair and Communist votes may have seemed plausible in 1948 or thereabout, but since then we have all learned a lot about all the terms of the equation, and discovered that there isn't any equation.

In the first place, until very recently, no nation at all ever "went Communist" in the sense of voters trooping to the polls to vote in, freely and in the presence of reasonable alternatives, a Communist government for any reason whatever, let alone in the hope that such a government would miraculously prove to be able to solve economic problems better than such governments have worked out in Russia, China and the rest. On the contrary, Communist governments have only come into power in the midst of or in the wake of vast wars and consequent social upheavals. In general the anti-Communist efforts of the Czar, the Kaiser, the Führer, the Mikado and Batista have produced more Communist states than have hunger and desperation. Hence, it is not unfair to conclude that the legislative selling of aid for underdeveloped nations on the ground that it will keep them from "going Communist" is an intellectual fraud and an attempt at a sort of blackmail: "Vote for the aid bill or watch West Zonta go Commie."

The fraud can be carried one step farther. We have learned since 1948 that the first stirrings of hope for a better life are much more likely to rouse people to violence and revolt than an unrelieved life of misery. In the United States nothing like the Black Panthers existed until after the civil rights legislation beginning in 1963. In that sense the Old Slave-Owners League is quite right: give 'em an inch and they want a mile: let 'em sit down for tuna-fish sandwiches in the 5 & 10 and the next thing you know they want to vote and run for office and carry on as if they were first-class citizens just like the rest of us. Translate that domestic experience into foreign terms and you conclude that, if the avoidance of Communist leanings is really your goal, you advocate no amelioration at all: the worse it is, the better it is. Any improvement in the lot of the masses of people in the underdeveloped nations is only the more likely to produce leaders and followers for radical social reorganizational movements easily labeled "Communist" by those who believe that General Motors is the general store of Scattergood Baines writ large and that the Kirov Leningrad Ballet Company is a slave labor camp writ small. Aid as anti-Communism is doubly a fraud because, in the first place, misery seems to have no causal connection with Communism except in the mind and heart of Karl Marx and, in the second, because some measure of relief from misery is needed in order to produce rebellious natives anxious to carry things a step or two farther.

The second main point, however, is worse than the first, as in the drinking song. The foreign aid impulse, all but unique in the world history of great powers, has been perhaps hopelessly corrupted by the amateurish attempt of its partisans to be junior Machiavellis, using the evil motive to pursue the good end and ending, inevitably, with the means becoming the end. There was a hope, at the end of the second great war of this century, that for once the victor in such a war would bend to the defeated to lift them up, would bend also to the innocent by-standers of the war, the captive peoples of Africa and Asia suddenly made free, and help them to become themselves and self-sufficient, insofar as that was within their power. That bending began to happen and it was abruptly shadowed by the anti-Communist motive.

Meanwhile, the problem of the underdeveloped nations has done nothing but get worse, nor does it show much promise of change in any other direction. The question is complicated, but some of the strands can and ought to be sorted out.

The colonial solution to the problem of the underde-veloped nations actually worked, within its own terms and its own severe limitations: the main limitation was that the colonial society was organized chiefly for the benefit of the occupying nation back home in Europe, but at least the society was given some sort of economic organization, its members allowed to work productively, and to keep some small part of their production for their own sustenance. When the colonial system broke down in the wake of World War II, the new nations, often totally artificial constructions set for the convenience of colonial administration found themselves unable, in many cases, to create a viable substitute for the former organization. Modern "miracle" medicine, largely introduced during and after World War II, proved to be a very mixed blessing: it led to fantastic increases of population by lowering the death rate dramatically, especially among infants, with none of the elaborate understructure of social-economic change which, in Europe and America, at once supported an increased population and gave that population the motive and the means to control its own growth. The problem of population growth in the under-developed countries is very far from being solved; any small, helpful gains in agriculture are immediately swallowed up by still further increases in population.

One would think that any rational person, confronting that situation, would see that hunger, present and future, is the great problem to be attacked by any means available, but especially, it seems obvious, by methods of increasing the yield per acre of foodstuffs. Yet, led by our military thinking about the world, American policy-makers have consistently deceived themselves that the main trouble with hunger is the opening it gives to Communism; hence, solutions to the troubles of the new nations have been sought in ways calculated to prevent the rise of Communist governments rather than in ways calculated to get people eating enough.

The junior Machiavelli approach to selling foreign aid as anti-Communism came as a brilliant stroke in some sort of high school debating enterprise, but was a catastrophe as far as foreign aid was concerned. The Kennedy Administration, under some compulsion, like many groups of liberal Democrats, to prove its staunch anti-Communism, came up with the concept of counterinsurgency as a pendant to the Peace Corps. The Peace Corps has provided some uplifting experiences for the tiny number of Americans involved but it has had virtually no effect on the worldwide problems of hunger and population control. Counterinsurgency, in contrast, has produced assorted small-time adventures in Latin America and the incredible adventure in Indochina that expanded so easily, naturally, almost unnoticed, from a handful of advisors in Saigon to an immense military operation all over that shattered peninsula.

The rascally Republicans for most of the twentieth century have made propaganda that the Democrats are the War Party. Wilson led us into World War I, Roosevelt into World War II, after both had been reelected on strong peace platforms. Truman led us into the Korean War, and Kennedy and Johnson into the Indochina War, neither of which shows much signs of ever getting over. In contrast, Republican Eisenhower promised that if elected, he would "go to Korea." He was, he did and he did succeed in winding that war down to no casualties and a relatively small permanent American occupation force. Richard Nixon, of all people, campaigned against the Kennedy-Johnson war in Vietnam, was elected, and did reverse the whole Democratic trend toward ever more troops, planes, ships, weapons and slogans. How come, if the Democrats are so liberal and enlightened and the Republicans are so crassly conservative, it is the Democrats who do, in fact, lead us into these wars, and the Republicans who, to some extent, deescalate them? Are the Democrats just unlucky? The Republicans just economical?

The great wars of the century are separate questions, involving the difficult task of taming the Germans, a task that has seemingly been accomplished at least for another couple of generations, and the industrialization of Japan, which is now also accomplished and working. But the two Asiatic anti-Communist wars are unquestionably Democratic wars. Particulars aside, one underlying reason has to be a felt need to prove the party's anti-Communism after its years of attack by the likes of Joe McCarthy—and Richard Nixon—as the Party of Treason. Poor old Tailgunner Joe, as McCarthy sometimes styled himself during political campaigns, was too spontaneous and disorganized a child of nature ever to have made much out of his really astoundingly successful anti-Communist presentation during the Truman and early Eisenhower years, but a case can be made that Richard Nixon rode his anti-Communism all the way to the Presidency. This parlaying of denunciations of Helen Gahagan Douglas printed on pink paper did not lead directly to the White House, as if by rousing the nation to the need for anti-Communism he was swept into power by the national fear of the Reds, but, rather, indirectly, by rousing the Democrats to their own need for a strengthened anti-Communist image and to the realization that you can't get much more anti-Communist than fighting a war. The Democratic overreaction in response to the early Nixon's anti-Communism produced, ultimately, Vietnam, which in turn produced Nixon as President and the voice of moderation in our anti-Communism. If this hypothesis of one man's climb to power interprets history correctly, Nixon is revealed as even sharper politically than he thought himself. You have to hand it to him, as the saying goes, and the Democrats did.

The final degradation of the American desire to further

some of the possibilities for peace and prosperity through programs of foreign aid occurred in the late winter-early spring of 1970. The country was just beginning to learn, in fragments torn with great difficulty from those military public servants who behave as if they owned the house, of our substantial involvement in Laos. A few months later we would find out about Cambodia, and the war would be rechristened the Indochina war, but at that time we were still speaking of the Vietnam war. Laos, we learned, had been subject to heavy bombing by our B-52s for several years. It had also been the scene of ground operations financed entirely by the United States and employing hired troops from several sources. The front, the cover agency, for the counterinsurgency, paramilitary headquarters was the AID mission in Laos, a pawn of the CIA. From the point of view of the spooks, it was doubtless a brilliant cover, allowing plenty of Americans to be seen in and around the cover installations and also giving the spook-generals an automatic allowance of beneficence. From the point of view of American long-range goals in the underdeveloped world, even including the anti-Communist goal, the cover was a catastrophe. On those terms it handed future Communist agitators in Asia, Africa and Latin America ready-made "proof" that any ameliorative American action in those areas is merely a front for secret military operations. Worse, it proved the same thing to Americans at home, especially those young Americans who, touched by the ideas of the Peace Corps and related domestic experiments, were once ready in larger numbers than budgets allowed for to devote some portions of their lives to such desperately needed work.

But in any terms, that Laotian cover was the final bankruptcy of the idea of foreign aid as an anti-Communist tool. As the Democrats demonstrated in Indochina, the ultimate anti-Communist expression is with a gun or a bomber. Like the hard-shell anti-Communists of the Birch Society, the idealistic Democrats and liberal Republicans of the original foreign aid coalition ended up playing soldier while the world's work remained to be done.

Through the Dark Glass

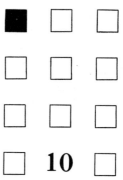

10

Except in primitive cultures, where religious ceremonies serve much the same purpose, war is about the best mirror of nations there is. It is an odd mirror, of course, at once a distorting glass like those encountered in amusement park fun houses, and a glass of prophecy, like those in old tales, speaking to the viewer and propounding riddles that tell the future.

There is nothing occult, however, about the explicatory relationship between war and society. War catches up the efforts of entire nations in a way that nothing else does. It intensifies those efforts, sharpens them, gives them a single focus. Certain social arrangements will often require considerable adjustment for war purposes and the adjusting will reveal strengths and weaknesses in the nation so in need of adjusting. The war effort, as is well known, invariably brings forth new machines and inventions that invariably affect the people that gave them birth. The Romans found out about war elephants from Hannibal, put them into circuses and they've been there ever since. Napoleon, anxious to have a provisioning system not wholly dependent on stealing all the food in sight, caused the food canning industry to come into existence, with the profound social result that whole generations since then have grown up, decayed and died without ever having tasted a real vegetable. In our own time, World War II developed radar and large airplanes to such an extent that now we have planes regularly stacked up over airports, the whine of jet engines everywhere, and the steady expansion of what must be, on balance, the most uncomfortable method of traveling long distances since the Conestoga Wagon.

These secondary, spinoff effects of war are so universally acknowledged and admired that some theorists, Hitler among them, have claimed that war is essential to the progress of the human race, providing a kind of forced march for the gifts of invention, a vigorous exercise of the applied intellect. The theory would seem to imply that if a long period of peace threatens to settle in, the patriotic citizen, or even the lover of humanity, will do his best to get something going somewhere, just to stir up a little more progress and avoid the awful stagnation inevitable if people spend their lives at work and play, sleep and love, without the moral and mental stimulation of a good war.

There probably is something in the felt connection between progress and war. That could be the root cause of the trouble with progress. It never quite shakes off the habits and inclinations of its origins. War, by definition, is carried on to kill a great many people and to make the lives of all others as dangerous and inconvenient as possible. Progress and its products, as we know too well, performs in much the same way whenever it is given its head. You have to watch progress every minute, or it reverts to type, turning motorcars into poison gas machines, and miracles of communication technology into instruments for filling the night air with Lawrence Welk.

War also produces attitudes and atmospheres for whole generations of the people engaged in it. The rich decadence of the Berlin of Bertolt Brecht and Kurt Weill got most of its peculiarities from the decisive defeat on the Western Front. While the officer corps, as such bodies are wont to do, nursed its resentment of "betrayal" on the home front, the soldiers and citizens became ever more certain that the whole leadership had been corrupt and incompetent: hence, for both sides, onward to Sodom.

The Napoleonic wars discovered, nourished and finally unleashed upon France the practitioners of that country's greatest and least appreciated art form, the energetic, ingenious and unscrupulous financial operator who gave French capitalism so much of its distinctive éclat.

In American history the great glass of war was the one that was burnished all over the country between the firing on Fort Sumter and the surrender at Appomattox. The

Civil War revealed and created a whole new America, that of the Industrial Age. The freeing of the slaves was important, God knows, but at the speed at which the practical implementation of the Emancipation Proclamation has taken place—"deliberate," the Supreme Court, 1954—obviously the organization of industry was vastly more important, giving shape to the nation for the next century and more. Buster Keaton, an authentic American artist of genius, instinctively selected the steam locomotive as the key symbol of the Civil War and he was quite right. Keaton's great Civil War picture, *The General,* takes its name from a locomotive that changes hands and that the comedian shepherds back to the Confederate forces. The picture is infinitely superior to *Gone with the Wind* and even to Griffiths' *Birth of a Nation* in terms of getting at the significance of the war. The latter is notable chiefly for its cinematic inventions, and film scholars regularly try to ignore his distinctly anti-Negro bias. Keaton, in contrast, goes right to the heart of the Civil War: the locomotive is what counts. The film is a secular ballet, as all Keaton's are, but the ballet is built around a man's relations with a machine, his endlessly inventive efforts to outguess the machine, to use the machine, to save the machine, to save himself from the machine. Besides its extraordinary comic beauty, *The General* is a correct analysis of what the Civil War was all about, and a devastatingly accurate summation of American industrial history since the war that started it all. The locomotive is still twisting around the bends, threatening to run over us, threatening to fall from the rickety bridge, threatening to stop altogether and become the enemy's while we Americans go scampering down the mountainside, leaping from the bluff, and teetering over trestles to keep the engine in hand, exactly like Buster Keaton, only not as graceful.

The Vietnam or Indochina war will assuredly contribute its mechanical share to our onward and upward strivings. Assuredly, too, that war reveals our nature and shapes our nature in the near future. Mechanically speaking, the helicopter is bound to come into its own after its yeoman service in "Nam." It will allow another generation to escape the impending permanent traffic jam on Seventh Avenue and the Mosholu Parkway, and possibly even give the generation after that the time needed to think up ways to escape the helicopter jam at the level of the fortieth floor. Here comes the chopper, the old rhyme has it, and welcome to it.

One of the great problems with the Pentagon has been occasioned by its adoption, early in the Vietnam war, of the Arthur Sylvester policy, which is summed up in the apothegm: Never tell the truth if a lie will serve as well. Sylvesterism, named for the Press Undersecretary who first sketched it out, ensures that you never know when they are lying and when they are telling the truth, which, presumably, is the point of the policy. One result is that there are, in press releases, any number of military miracles with an easy and obvious adaptation to civilian life but you can't tell whether they really exist or not. They could so easily have been mere figments of a dull day in the Pentagon press when somebody felt the need to say something about something, it hardly mattered what. One such announcement, a couple of years back, which could as easily be true as false, concerned another miracle weapon with which the war was to be won any minute, as soon as we had got to the light at the end of the tunnel and finished turning the corner we were half way around already. The weapon was the "Cong Smeller," and it'll be a best seller when it gets demobilized—assuming it ever existed. The Cong Smeller was based on the old-fashioned cockroach, thus pressing into active service an ancient companion of soldiers. The Army discovered, or claimed to have discovered, that certain cockroaches are hypersensitive to the smells of the unwashed human body. Since by definition Americans are hyperwashed and the South Vietnamese are Americans in training, the cockroaches, the Army said—and surely the Army should know—react only to the smells of the Viet Cong hiding in the underbrush. The cockroaches, held out on the ends of sticks, were expected to register the near presence of the hated insurgents by wiggling their antennae in the appropriate direction, rather like a water douser's wand taking a dip when passed over a subterranean spring.

Back in civilian life, in the age that has created and endured the Indochina war, the Smeller can be enormously useful. White suburbanites can maintain their faithful cockroaches permanently pointed in the direction of the inner city to give distant early warning of the approach of minority groups or even of their own freaky children, both members of the Great Unwashed, as such people were called in an age more innocent than any we have known for some time.

Beyond the level of miraculous cockroaches and traffic-eluding helicopters, the mirror of the war reflects the society in two ways at once, present and future, neither of them very flattering.

To begin with, there is the depressing fact that we have lost the war and don't even know it. The Henry Kissinger formulation applies: A conventional army has to win or it has lost, while a guerrilla force wins as long as it has not lost. We Americans are highly conventional in battle as elsewhere and we have not won; the enemy is totally guerrilla and it has not lost. Yet still we hang on there, simply unable to believe that any nation as big as ours, with as many nuclear warheads in the old stockpiles, and as many think tanks on tap, could ever lose. It used to be that when a nation lost a war the victorious enemy arrived in Tokyo Bay, at Potsdam, or at Appomattox or Yorktown to communicate the news and dictate the terms. The great advantage of that system, for the loser, was that he could accept reality and get on with the future. The United States lost the war in Vietnam round about 1965, when the joint chiefs and their chief assistants and assistant chiefs were all being blinded by the light at the end of the tunnel. Yet we have stayed on, throwing money down the drain and killing our youth (and Vietnamese, South and North) by the thousands simply because the chiefs and their chums are too dumb to recognize defeat unless someone arrives and asks for their swords.

Defeat in war is a new thing for the United States, but it reflects and presages a whole new age of defeat on many other fronts. The age has already begun and is certain to get worse year by year. The bright midday of science and technology, we are only now starting to learn, passed some time ago. We grope through a twilight distinguished everywhere by the revival of the incantatory method of conjuring up results. The results don't always appear; indeed, they usually do not, but the method does lead to a rich repertoire of incantations.

In Vietnam, it will be recalled by anyone unfortunate enough to have piled up their daily newspapers during the long years of that war, American policy moved regularly from incantation to incantation. When it was agreed that one magical formula hadn't worked, the incantatory service—perhaps aided by a think tank or two—produced on schedule a new one. Anyone, even a nonnewspaper reader, is bound to remember some of them: the Hamlet program, which turned out to have more to do with the Prince of Denmark than was at first thought; the campaign to win the minds and the hearts of the people; the bombing of the Ho Chi Minh trail in several countries, thus interdicting the flow of vital supplies to the insurgents; the Democratic elections, designed to give the people a stake in their country; the Land Reform, designed to give the people another stake in their country; Vietnamization, followed swiftly by Cambodianization; and others too numerous and depressing to recall. The programs were varied in scope, in effort, in field of operations and area of application, but they all had one thing in common: every one of them was equipped with a dandy new name and a first-class press release explaining how it would win the war. As time went by and the war went on, some cynics concluded that the name and the press release were all the shiny program had.

This is probably not true, or at least not true of *all* of them. But it does seem true that most of them were conceived in terms of the names and the press releases, which is to say they were all examples of the incantatory method, the system by which the Southwest Indians invoke the heavens to open and pour down rain, Yankee sailors conjured up a wind, and Madison Avenue conjure-men to this day get clothes whiter-than-white and cleaner-than-clean.

It was discovered by America's first great student of advertising, a scholar still unsurpassed in the depth of his insights, Fred Allen, that our modern incantations are not really addressed to the gods whose names they repeat, nor yet to the presumed faithful huddling in the nave of the washday church waiting for the miracle of super-whiteness to gleam from the dirty old jockey shorts, but rather to the mind and the heart of the advertiser himself, the man who pays the bills, or "sponsor," as he was called in Allen's day. The situation is something like one that is reflected in those Flemish and Venetian paintings, wherein the donor of the painting and his family are being presented to the Virgin Mary and other dignitaries by angels or appropriate saints. In the same fashion, Allen noticed, the costly advertisements of radio—and, later, of television—are actually directed to the self-esteem of the man who hires the creator of the ads. Obviously, if anyone believed the remarkable claims made in word and image about soap powders, no American husband would leave his wife alone in the house on washday, at least until the sexual revolution is rather more advanced than it is now. The multiple orgasms produced in housewives on television as they see their whiter-than-whites emerge from the machine are clearly not intended to sell the soap chips, but to flatter the chairman of the board. This is reasonable enough; what the hell, if you are a board chairman you're entitled to a certain amount of sexual novelty. If he didn't get it with his soap chips, he might be molesting little girls in parks. Or little boys.

In the war in Indochina, too, the endlessly changing incantations certainly are not directed to the presumed objects of their concern, the minds and the hearts and all that; still less to the longer-range goal of winning the war. They are directed, the student must conclude, solely and exclusively to the joint chiefs of staff and their fellow communicants in that religion. It makes them feel good that there is a Hamlet program, that the Vietnamese are now Democratic landowners instead of serfs defrauded by their leaders, and so on. The fact that any such changes as these would involve a vast social revolution which would alienate almost every Vietnamese official loyal to America (and at the same time outflank the Communists), can most easily be gotten around not by doing the things but by proclaiming them. Like the chairman of the board of Procter & Gamble or General Motors, the joint chiefs don't need a sex life; all they have to do is turn on their own commercials.

Environment has become a fashionable concern in recent years, neatly replacing civil rights long before the basic problems of the civil rights "revolution" are remotely solved. Although one can expect it to be dropped when the going gets tough (as it must, to mean anything), in the meantime it is enormously useful for the incantation makers of the left. Environment, ecology, pollution, these are our new magic words, and again we are not surprised that the reality turns up in Vietnam in clearer, more sharply focused form, than back in the homeland—"the world," as the soldiers say. Back in that homeland, we are only now coming to grips with the shattering truth that science destroys as readily as it creates, that the technology on which we have increasingly lived high for decades extracts a huge toll from that nature which is the only one we have. Fossil fuels fill the air with poison and the coastal seas with goo. Birds die, citizens wax irate with Standard Oil. For the sake of a mindless technology we mindlessly pollute the water we drink, the air we breathe, the ground we need to live. Appropriately enough, in Vietnam, we have unleashed, as one of our numerous miracle weapons, the concept of defoliation, the stripping of leaves off the trees and bushes for the sake of stripping off the leaves. Back in the world, there was always some pretense that the killing of nature was accomplishing some other good. You can't make omelets without breaking the eggs, nor electricity without befouling the air. In Vietnam it was found possible to destroy the trees with no corresponding technological gain whatever. There was said to be a gain in security, but this is one of those vague values impossible to prove. Certainly it wasn't proved by the immediate destruction of the Viet Cong and the North Vietnamese after the defoliation of former greenery in South Vietnam. If, as increasingly appears to be the case, the real, inner, soul-purpose of technology is to make life as grim and unpleasant as possible, to destroy nature for the sake of destroying nature, the defoliation program was a major leap forward and we Americans may soon expect to see it applied in our backyards.

Vietnam has brought into very sharp focus another aspect of the way we live now, one generally not understood until the war more or less threw it in our faces. The terrible fact is that technology itself is a big flop. We do not ask technology to produce poetry or paintings, sonnets or sonatas, any of the things that really make life worth living. We ask it only to produce that which forms a kind of base on which we can stand in order to begin to live. We ask technology, for example, for transportation, for machines of many kinds, for communication, for the lever, the pulley and the inclined plane raised to the hundredth or so power. It is not, when you think of it, a frightfully demanding request of a line of work that has consistently billed itself as the outline of a brave new world. All we want is a good servant. It is more than technology can deliver. The most damning indictment of the whole, gaudy technological revolution is not that it substitutes material values for spiritual ones or any of that Mary Shelley stuff. The basic trouble with technology is simply that it doesn't work. Like Prohibition, it's a great experiment, but it just hasn't panned out.

Anyone who has had, for example, a credit card with an oil company or a charge account with a department store which has gone over to computerized accounting knows the protracted agony it is to deal with those idiot machines. It is not so much that they cannot do sums correctly as that it is absolutely impossible to communicate their error to them. They continue, month after month, to send in the same bill, augmented by each month's fraction of the eighteen percent per annum needed to support the machines, in total disregard of the customer's protest. The income tax department relies on the same machines and gobbles up vast portions of the citizen-taxpayer's time, mental energy and money before it allows a human being to intervene and the human being, invariably, remarks, "Oh, yes, quite right, two and two do make four, don't they?" That perception is beyond the grasp of the allegedly ninth-generation "sophisticated" computers. Or try getting a faulty television set to work at less than the cost of a new set. Or a car. Or what you will.

There was a time—it seems only yesterday—when humanist savants would argue that the machines were giving us mechanical perfection but robbing us of our souls. Such debates are now a luxury not quite imaginable by people who actually own machines or are in the thrall of those owned by Lord & Taylor or the Internal Revenue Service. No one except the extraordinarily naive ever believed that machines would open the gates to the New Paradise, but the silly things don't even work on their own silly terms. They can't heat a pot of water for tea without burning down the house, or add up a column of figures without, somehow, getting it wrong.

The principle applies and is raised by more than a power or two in the war in Vietnam. Nothing has worked. The poor old C–5, another miracle airplane that was to cut costs, win wars and be the biggest and best ever conceived and built, is a fair example. It ran about fifty percent over estimated costs. Its wings developed cracks.

At its dedication, a wheel fell off, for no particular reason. Finally, the prototype model, the first one built, simply blew itself up, bang, good-by, no sabotage, no enemy action, no nothing, just plain old techno-incompetence, the curse of the race.

The young, God bless them, can afford to argue the morality and immorality of our performance in Vietnam. To the quietly aging, the question of the morality of it all doesn't even arise until the technocrats learn how to do whatever it is they are trying to do. Like trying to make a phone call in New York or an air voyage from New York to Washington, the war in Vietnam is not moral tragedy but slapstick farce.

The Permawar

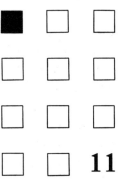

The main trouble with wars, from the point of view of a military man, is that sooner or later, do what you will, they are over. They end. The nation gets on to other things. The news programs start showing pictures of civilian activities. The national budget shifts from military expenditures to those of peace. The number of men under arms is reduced and consequently so is the number and rank of commissioned officers needed to command them. Yesterday's generals find themselves lucky to be majors. The household staff is reduced to one all-around driver-yardman, often merely a corporal. The officers'

club bar cuts back on its hours and the commissary on its imported gourmet items. War may be hell, but peace is no bargain either, from the point of view of a military man.

Such, at least, used to be the traditional pattern, but that has now changed. The military, tired of the endless ups and downs of fortune as wars developed, raged and died away, have solved the problem. They have invented the Permawar.

Vietnam was the tryout, the out-of-town opening for the Permawar. It was a smashing success. Most Americans now think of Vietnam as a colossal failure, but that's because they think of wars in conventional, civilian terms. In those terms wars are fought to gain specific goals—the liberation of a country from a conqueror, the securing of trade routes, the capture of valuable treasure of some sort. The successful war is the war that achieves its goals as efficiently, economically and swiftly as possible, like the successful surgical operation and the successful symphony. From that limited viewpoint, it is true, Vietnam is a hideous failure. The government we went in there to save was assassinated long ago, apparently with our connivance. We went in to allow the South to manage its own affairs without interference from the North, but in fact our "elected" government turned out to be headed by Northerners, Thieu and Ky, who proved to be not unsympathetic to the interests of their countrymen from up north. We went in to save the country itself and its hardworking, long-suffering peasantry and have inflicted on both such suffering as no Asiatic peasantry has endured in centuries. We have burned crops, destroyed villages, broken up families, tortured suspected enemy sympathizers and killed civilians out of hand, all in order to save them. To pursue this course, we have escalated the war to a level of annual expenditure slightly surpassing, in 1968, the top level of World War II. We have conscripted hundreds of thousands of our youth, killing many, wounding more, driving some to flee the country and many others into long-term alienation from the country. It is difficult for an American civilian to add all this up to anything more than utter failure.

In military terms, however, most of the items, especially the vast expenditures, have to be classed as stunning successes. To raise a "brush-fire war" in a remote corner of the world up to the expenditure level of the greatest war in history is no small achievement. But to keep the war going as long as it has been kept going was an achievement even more remarkable—and the beginning of the Permawar.

Most wars have been started with trumpets and banners, so that people knew they were going on. This, in Permawar theory, was their initial mistake. The trumpets and banners rallied people round and did make for a certain gratifying adulation, in song and speech, of the nation's military men. But that momentary gratification was purchased at the cost of having the whole nation know that a war was on and expect some sort of conclusion on some loose schedule within their lifetimes.

Permawar avoids that popular knowledge and those popular expectations by beginning wars surreptitiously. This sounds like a hard thing to do, like sneaking an elephant into the house without disturbing the bridge party in the living room, but it proved amazingly easy in Vietnam. The surreptitious approach there was so dazzlingly successful that to this day no one really knows exactly when the war began. Some of its origins go back to the desperate French effort to hang onto its rich colony of Indochina, yet when the French collapsed at Dien Bien Phu, the Americans did not immediately pick up the torch. We had been lending or giving the French weapons to resist the misguided efforts of the Indochinese to run Indochina. When the French surrendered, we transferred the weapons and added a few more to the imperial forces of the Vietnamese emperor, Bao Dai. To explain and service the weapons and other equipment, we sent along American technicians. To protect the technicians we began sending in a few troops—rather like the Marines outside our embassies around the world, it was thought by anyone who happened to think about it at all.

The government changed. The technicians began helping the soldiers of the new government and more troops were required to protect the technicians. We had an "advisory" force present, and more and more advice seemed to be required. It came. As late as the Presidential campaign of 1964, President Johnson could still say with a straight face that American boys were not going to do the fighting that ought to be done by Asian boys. The American boys could, however, give advice to the Asian boys and teach by example how to aim, fire, search and destroy, pacify and clear. The incident in the Tonkin Gulf—if there was an incident in the Tonkin

Gulf—was the first indication most Americans had that we were at war over there, but the North Vietnamese, obviously, had taken it for granted for some time. The incident—if there was one—was generally accepted as a latter-day Pearl Harbor or sinking of the Maine or the Lusitania. We are accustomed to having our foreign wars open with a naval attack of some sort and we accepted this as traditional with no serious question about what our advisory forces were up to in the Gulf in the first place. Senator Fulbright, who lived to regret it, engineered a Tonkin Resolution through the Senate, authorizing the President to take whatever steps he deemed appropriate. That document is the only thing remotely resembling a declaration of war that this war has ever had. On that authority, the big bombing of the North began and spread rapidly through the other countries. On that authority Nixon based the Cambodian "incursion" of spring, 1970, which promptly turned two thirds of that country over to the local Communist insurgents and never did uncover the Viet Cong headquarters supposedly located just over the border. Against that background the Nixon peace offensive of autumn, 1970, had a certain hollowness in its ring which became positively cavernous with the leaking of a CIA report that the South Vietnamese government had been infiltrated by thirty thousand Communists. The Reds were said to have adopted this course because they were unable to stand up on the battlefield to the success of the "Vietnamization" program of the current incantations. But what the leak really meant was that when Vietnamization failed, as it was bound to, the United States would be forced to stay on in Indochina to save the South Vietnamese government from itself. In short, Permawar.

The Cambodian incursion itself set up a sort of battlefield revolving door that might also be essential to the Permawar. The Americans withdrew from South Vietnam to incur into Cambodia. With Laos also extremely eligible for a full-scale incursion, any Joint Chief with half a brain can keep the war going indefinitely by shifting from one country to another in pursuit of the wily insurgents, keeping as his ace up the sleeve the CIA's report that the government we fight to defend is already heavily Communist. It would require higher mathematics than we have to calculate all the possibilities for Permawar created by the very steps said to be ending the Indochina war. But even if it should, through some mischance, come to a temporary end in the near future, it will still have had the longest run of any war in our history, which isn't bad for a war without James Montgomery Flagg or Irving Berlin. That's Permawar.

Future possibilities of Permawar exist also in the Middle East, in Africa and, most of all at the moment, in Latin America. Chile, with the first elected Marxist government in history, and Bolivia, with its very generals turning Left, are prime areas for Permawar to set in as the land owners and foreign investors begin to be hurt from serious land reform, set up counter governments with some shreds of legitimacy, and enlist the advisory help of the anti-Communists to the north. The formula is clear and is always open to local variations.

Permawar as developed in Indochina is based on the

assumption that there is a specter in the world and it is Communism, a single, international force, directed from Moscow or Peking, out to encompass the destruction of the United States by any means possible but especially by getting Communist governments into power in tiny, impoverished, out-of-the-way countries whose peoples have thrown off their European colonial rulers or, it may be, their native exploiters. The "legitimate," i.e. anti-Communist, governments deserve our support because they are anti-Communist. As that help proves futile, it is increased. As the increase is attacked, it is "hardened," or protected by other forces. Soon it is directly and forcefully attacked and the attack becomes the *causus belli* for a war already several years old. The aims of the war may shift wildly as it proceeds and these shifts reveal in startling clarity that the real aim of the war is to have a war. The final argument in Indochina, for a year or so before the Vietnamization program, was that we had to keep our troops in Vietnam in order to protect our troops in Vietnam. The same sequence can easily be duplicated in the South American highlands and doubtless will be.

But in the curious world of the paper condottieri and the unfree-nonenterprisers of the Pentagon, the actual shooting, fighting and dying war out there in the boonies somewhere is only the shadow, the visible sign, and the validation of the real Permawar, the one that rages without respite or truce in the think tanks, the executive offices and the congressional hearing rooms. The real Permawar is the one of ever-new, more elaborate, more lethal, more expensive, more absolutely essential, weapons systems. Like the Permawar of ground and aerial combat, the

Permawar of think tank, arms factory and committee room has its own patterns already well developed, patterns in some ways similar to those of a surreptitious shooting war.

The principal common bond is the fait accompli.

In the Permawar properly so-called, the one out there with the Gooks in the boonies, by applying the principle of counterinsurgency, the American military command is able to get quite a nice little war going for as long as three or four, possibly five, years, before anyone back in the world knows it is happening at all. The technique is military aid for our democratic allies, plus instructors to go with the hardware and protectors to guard the instructors. Raise that gradually to the tenth power and you are in business. Then, as press and public—and perhaps even President—slowly comprehend that there is actually a good deal of shooting going on over there, the purpose of the operation is switched to the defense of American boys. This is a goal almost no one will oppose, and few will even have the wit, at the moment of peril, to point out that one good way to defend American boys is to bring them home. By similar shifts of motive, of geography, of the nature—or even the identity—of the enemy, of war aims, and of tactics and strategy, the war can be kept going indefinitely.

Meanwhile, back at the think tank, the same basic use of the fait accompli is now a standard operating procedure, a reflex style like a tennis player's return of service. No weapon or weapons system is ever presented initially as costing anything within artillery range of its final price. Its final price, for that matter, is ascertainable, if at all, only after monumentally difficult prying out and sorting out of figures. Systems begin small and grow large, increasing their costs geometrically rather than arithmetically as they grow. When Congress at large finds out that something new is in the works, a substantial investment has already been made and it seems silly, just on ordinary business management terms, to throw that away. So the investment increases and every increment is a powerful argument, all by itself, that the commitment itself is correct. The time warp, that invaluable concept from science fiction, comes into play here in both directions at once. Congress and the country are always dealing with military extravagance of at least a year or so ago: it is too late to do anything about it now and better to save what we can than scrap the whole investment. On the other hand, the paper condottieri are always dealing in futures, like the men in the grain pit, and no one is more susceptible to future shock than a Congressman facing reelection within the foreseeable. Work on the moondust machine has to begin now because by the time we definitely know one way or the other that the Russians have one, it will be too late. As in the boonies, so the loonies of R & D are capable of infinite flexibility of motive and scope. The ABM, the variously called Sentinel or Safeguard System, has been the prime example in recent years. Originally merchandised as a defense of our cities against the Yellow Peril of Peking, it modulated easily into a defense of our own missile sites against the Russians, and ended, brilliantly, as an actual instrument of disarmament in the minds of the Congressmen who signed the check. The real reason the system had to be built, of course, was simply that it could be built.

That sort of war, too, can go on forever. Through the astute use of the time warp, the awful threat of peace and the worse one of disarmament are almost automatically held at bay. Disarmament requires a mutual suspension of disbelief that is temporally impossible, since decisions on fantasy arms of the future have to be made long before disarmament discussions begin, and the arms themselves brought to reality as a sort of background chuckle to any possible conversations toward sanity. From the condottieri point of view, there must have been something deeply satisfying in the coincidence, as it was assumed to be, of China, Russia and the United States all three celebrating the silver anniversary of the United Nations with mammoth nuclear explosions. Only testing, Dag.

Our country has become a military dictatorship in its own peculiar American way. We think of the term as meaning tanks around the Presidential palace at dawn and gaudy uniforms decked with bandoliers striding up the staircase to the balcony and the microphones. But that isn't our way. We operate in boardrooms and in balance sheets and it is in those quiet shelters that the change has taken place. Unlike conventional military dictatorships, ours is not personal. The Joint Chiefs go by like trolley cars. Again, the principle is American, the standard, interchangeable parts system invented by Eli Whitney for, appropriately enough, a gun factory. Our version of the military dictatorship is so much our own that the traditional sign of the phenomenon, armed soldiers on street corners, brings only relief to the hearts of honest citizens when it appears during civil disturbances. The reality exists not in those friendly troops helping old ladies across the street, but in the percentage of the national budget—"Rock bottom!" The Pentagon—given over to arms in a time of peace and in the permanent block that the arms community presents to the cause of peace in the world, the cause of humanity abroad, and the pursuit of happiness for all at home.

There has been some resistance to all this, of course, but the new military establishment has become so extremely flexible when it wants to be that it is well advanced in the complicated process of turning the resistance to its own purposes. Youth—ah, youth—has aligned itself very vocally against the draft and in so doing has missed the point. The draft will probably go. It is already an aim of the Nixon Administration to end the draft, or at least end its operation, a slightly different thing. But its going will mean, on the one hand, the end of about ninety percent of the antimilitary agitation and, on the other, a substantial raise for all hands to attract enough recruits to make up an all-volunteer army, with the biggest raises, as always, going to the generals and master sergeants who are already in for life anyway. It is a beautiful maneuver, like Japanese wrestling, right up there with deploying the ABM in the cause of disarmament.

That military flexibility, alas, is only tactical. The military destiny and the destiny of militarist nations that survive long enough to meet it was painted long ago by El Greco in a church in Toledo, the city of steel. In the

Burial of Count Orgaz, whatever ectoplasmic ectasies are going on in heaven above, down below on the Spanish earth, the armed men are turning into their own armor. And so are we.

Upon the death of the late-lamented Gamal Abdel Nasser, it was widely remarked that he had done much to promote the ruin of his country despite his early hopes of Arab Socialism and a Pan-Arab Union and a general amelioration of the long-endured plight of some of the world's most exploited, neglected and downtrodden people. There was general agreement that he blew his chances and those of his country by a fatal passion for military adventures beyond his borders, especially the still incredible six-day war of 1967. There was agreement too that that predilection for military shenanigans over the detailed and worrisome efforts required to build a new society is one of the great weaknesses of many leaders in the emerging nations. The military way seems easy and direct to them and thus seduces them away when they ought to be at home with the slide rule and the county agricultural agent. Their problem, of course, is that they lack the advantages of Western, industrialized education, so they can't see those things.

Poor Nasser. It's all true, of course, but he is so far from being alone and his profound errors of military adventurism are so far from being the invention of the Third World. Like the boy in the fable, the student nations do what their masters do instead of what they say.

We play soldier in the end—and to the end—because it is easier than working.